FIRST,
THEY WERE
CHILDREN

ORIGIN STORIES OF 7 PEOPLE
WHO CHANGED THE WORLD

**Bill Gates – Steve Jobs – Walt Disney – Albert Einstein
Henry Ford – Nikola Tesla – Thomas Edison**

Copyright © 2018 **David Butler**

Table of Contents

Who Were They as Children?

Here are stories of seven people who changed the world. We're all familiar with their adult accomplishments, but who were they as children? What was childhood like for them, their friends, their families, and their teachers?

Hopefully, by following the childhoods of these remarkable people, we'll better understand our own children, and even our own childhoods. Sometimes, fitting in is difficult for a child, but the problem might not be the square peg, but rather, the round hole.

Here's a brief description of the source of my own curiosity about this subject. By the time my first-born son was ready to start kindergarten, he was brilliant to the point that other people often commented on it to his mother and me. At five years old, he could add up strings of three-digit numbers in his head, mentally convert between binary and decimal, and could read any book fluently and with expression.

I only tell you this because I want you to understand my total shock when his second-grade teacher recommended putting him back a grade.

"This makes no sense because Jason's obviously very smart," I protested. "How can you say he's not ready for second-grade?" "I don't think Jason is mature enough yet. He's constantly fidgeting at his desk or talking to other students," she answered. "That's why I propose we move him back to first-grade. In my opinion this will be best for him in the long run."

I pleaded with the teacher to reconsider and told her that he's probably just bored. I told her that Jason cried when he heard about this, and thought this meant he was too "stupid" to stay with his friends in second grade.

This teacher had a combined class that was split down the middle into a second and third-grade section, so asked her if she could first let Jason temporarily join the third-grade side of her class.

It was agreed that this could be tried as an experiment for one month, and this is what's written in the teacher-parent conference report she handed me four months later. "Jason is working at 3rd grade level and is doing a fine job. He is a conscientious student and wants to do his best at all times. He grasps concepts quickly and seeks additional information."

Three months later, Jason was transferred to the gifted program where he continued to excel.

What I learned from this experience was that busy and well-meaning teachers can easily mistake some unusual behaviors for disabilities. With this realization came the sad realization that many other children are probably being similarly mislabeled, and may also end up convinced there's something wrong with them.

Although I lost Jason to leukemia when he was nine years old, I watched his two younger brothers, Austin and Travis, endure similar challenges in school. Both were bright boys, but they also struggled with classwork, repeatedly bringing home report cards loaded with Ds and Fs, especially after elementary school when the gifted course ran out. None-the-less, today they are extremely successful adults, and run a popular educational business at teaching.com, helping millions of children world-wide enjoy learning.

It's this experience with my children and the standard school system that led me to wonder what some of the famous icons of history must have gone through while growing up. How were they perceived when they were children? How did they personally cope with or fit into their educational systems? And what were they like as children? That is, what traits or experiences did they share, and is there a way to recognize these types of special talents early on?

Answering these questions is the goal of this book. Here are stories of seven people who changed the world. We're all familiar with their remarkable accomplishments as adults, but it's difficult to even imagine them as children.

What would such childhoods have been like? What would it have been like for them and for their families? What led them to become such enormous successes in their chosen endeavors?

Surprisingly, I was unable to find a book specifically exploring the childhoods of these people. Of course, I found many biographies about them, but none spent much time on their childhoods. Each book generally spent only the most perfunctory attention to the early part of their lives, before jumping quickly into the supposedly more "important" parts.

The only books I found that focused on them as children were books specifically written for children, as if only a child would be interested in the life of a child.

Several biographies though did contain small snippets of their childhoods. By collecting and comparing these stories with each other as well as with other online research, I was able to verify and order these accounts into the more complete childhood biographies in this book.

Through the resulting stories, you'll be able to understand and know these individuals on the deepest level, because to know someone's childhood, is to know the foundations of their personalities, and the values and desires that drive them throughout their lives.

It gives you a peek into the most intimate part of these otherwise well-known lives. It shows how they grew from simple childhoods into incredible adulthoods, how they were the same as other children — and how they were different.

We probably think we know these people, in that we know they're brilliant and we know how they changed the world, but how did they get that way? How did they develop the kind of drive, imagination, and passion that such accomplishments must have required?

Although each of these children came from different backgrounds and family environments, you'll notice that by around the age of seven or eight, they all seemed to have developed a particular and unique interest that they were unable to let go of.

Even though these people were brilliant and able to see way beyond the typical horizons most of us live within, as children they could also easily be misunderstood.

Their drive and passion often caused them to be impatient with standard education techniques and sometimes led them to be misunderstood or mislabeled as trouble-makers or even learning-disabled.

These people had a large part in fashioning the modern world we inhabit today, a world which is light-years away from our childhoods and theirs. It's easy to take many of today's comforts and conveniences for granted, but difficult to imagine how life would be without the inventions, discoveries, and products these people gave us.

Above, clockwise from the left, are the childhood faces of the seven people in this book: Henry Ford, Steve Jobs, Thomas Edison, Walt Disney, Albert Einstein, Bill Gates, and Nikola Tesla.

I decided to only include people who were both household names and who truly changed the world. These are people we're already familiar with and they're people who have changed this world to the extent that if you were to travel to another planet exactly like Earth, except that the discoveries and inventions of one of these people did not exist, you'd hardly recognize the place!

For example, try to imagine our world without the power of Tesla's AC electricity, or the abundant modern technology based on Einstein's incredible theories, or the modern comforts affordably manufactured by Ford's mass-production efficiencies.

Since the goal of this book is to compare their childhoods, note that these biographies only cover their first two decades. Each story closes shortly before their 21st birthday, at a more or less transitional moment in their lives.

We'll leave each of them at this point in time when they've found their direction and begun the more famous and familiar portions of their lives. Here we'll only focus on those early formative years, to see how they got from point A to point B. Although later points C, D, E, etc. are still fascinating, they generally continue to follow the earlier direction rooted in childhood. It's the discovery and understanding of these paths, that is the goal of this book.

To more easily identify with these children, the stories have been arranged in reverse-chronological order, beginning with the world we're more familiar with, and then stepping story-by-story back through time.

I think you're going to be surprised and intrigued by the childhood biographies of these game-changers. If you're raising children, have grown children, or have ever been a child, you're going to enjoy reading and sharing these stories.

Individually, these childhood biographies give important glimpses into who these people really are and how they went from small children to giants of history. Together, these stories give an important and useful overview into how these personalities formed: what turned a young Thomas into "Edison" or little Albert into "Einstein."

They're also full of many insightful and surprising anecdotes and experiences. A few examples:

Bill Gates, Age 7: Young Bill had already developed a love of reading and the ability to remember practically everything. Much of his remarkable reading proficiency grew from an uncommonly competitive nature, driving him to win the summer reading contests at his school.

Steve Jobs, Age 5: Fascinated by the craftsmanship and attention to detail his father put into restoring cars, Steve was a budding product developer. His father stressed that every part of a project should be well-made with precision and care, even those that no one would see.

Walt Disney, Age 8: When his family had to leave the small idyllic town of Marceline and move to Kansas City, Missouri, the only thing little Walt liked about their new home was that it was close to the Fairmount amusement park. Although he couldn't afford to get in, he loved to stand at the fence and stare into this "fairyland."

Albert Einstein, Age 8: Already in touch with the mysteries of math, young Albert would become so immersed in solving his mathematical problems that his sister said he looked like an absent-minded Buddha sitting lost in thought in a trancelike state.

Henry Ford, Age 7: Industrious Henry developed unique hinges that allowed him to open farm gates without getting off his wagon. The practical young boy was always devising easier ways to get his chores done. He hated farm work, but was especially repelled by inefficient and wasted effort.

Nikola Tesla enjoyed watching his mother work around their house and farm throughout his childhood. He was fascinated with her inventiveness, as she created many new and ingenious devices to replace the old tools that hadn't changed in centuries.

Thomas Edison was a rather ordinary child, but when he started school, he had trouble paying attention. Chances are he may have suffered from attention deficit disorder or dyslexia. His teacher told Thomas's mother that her son must have some sort of insurmountable mental challenge, and that it would be impossible to teach him anything.

So now, take a fresh new look into these well-known lives — but little-known childhoods, to discover many surprising insights and clues to these unique characters.

If you'd like to share your impressions about these stories, I'd certainly love hearing from you, either by email or in a book review on Amazon.

Thanks for reading.

David Butler

email@davidbutler.us

Bill Gates

October 28, 1955 – Present

People overestimate what they can do in one year and underestimate what they can do in ten.
— Bill Gates

On April 4, 1975, Bill Gates and his friend Paul Allen launched a small company called Microsoft. It soon grew into the largest company in the world, producing an operating system that ran 90 percent of the world's computers, and making computers easier and more productive through the simple graphical interface of Windows and through the integrated suite of Office tools.

By 1992, at the age of 37, Bill Gates was the richest man in the world. Since then, he has given away more than $37 billion to numerous charities. But even this incredible generosity still pales alongside the wealth of improvements in people's lives that have resulted from placing the power of computing into the hands of so many people.

By creating an operating system that made affordable computers more accessible to everyday users, Bill Gates unleashed the innovative energy of millions, who then used these computers to generate, analyze, and spread information on a scale never before possible.

This new wide-spread capacity to process, transfer, and store information rapidly and efficiently led to break-throughs which are improving and saving millions of lives a year.

Of course, many others have contributed to the computer revolution, but more than anyone, Bill Gates is responsible for bringing the power of computing to the masses. Without his hard-driving passion to excel and his extremely competitive nature, we'd likely be living in a terribly different world today: one still waiting for the many scientific, technological, agricultural, medical, and communication breakthroughs we now take for granted.

The personal computer revolution unleashed a burst of ingenuity, and at the epicenter of this explosion, was a boy pursuing his firmly held childhood conviction that all successes would be rewarded.

~~~

Friday, October 28, 1955

By 1955, consumerism was firmly rooted in America. This was the year McDonald's built their first restaurant, and Coca-Cola began selling soda in cans. Elvis Presley and Chuck Berry dominated the radio waves, and 70 percent of American families owned a car.

But no one owned a computer. That would soon change.

In Seattle, Washington, shortly after 9 p.m., William Henry Gates III was born to William Henry Gates II and Mary Maxwell Gates.

Mary Maxwell was an outgoing and athletic Seattle native of Scotch-Irish descent. She participated in student affairs while attending the University of Washington and after graduating, worked as a teacher. Once she became a mother, Mary quit teaching but stayed involved in her volunteer activities.

William Henry Gates II, was of English-German descent, and was born in Bremerton, Washington. After serving in the army during World War II, William attended the University of Washington as a promising if somewhat shy law student. William and Mary met at the university and married in 1951.

William III was their second child. His sister Kristianne (Kristi) was two years older. A younger sister, Elizabeth (Libby), was born nine years later.

At home, young William was called Little Bill, or Trey. Trey is a cardplayer's term for three. His grandmother gave him the nickname to avoid confusion when speaking to the father or son, and Trey is what the family usually called him. To the rest of the world, he would become known as Bill Gates and his father as Bill Gates Sr.

Bill was an active child. As an infant, he loved rocking back and forth in his cradle. Later, his parents gave him a rocking horse, on which he would sit and rock for hours. His parents thought he was hyperactive and hoped the rocking horse would calm him down, but Bill later explained he enjoyed rocking because it helped him think.

Before Bill was old enough for school, Mary took him with her when she did volunteer work. He accompanied her as she made presentations at various schools in Seattle and he became accustomed to being in classrooms at an early age.

When Bill started school, since his birthday was in October, he was the youngest in his class. He was also small for his age, but he was ready for school and excelled as a student.

Bill also soon excelled at reading. His teachers gave reading lists of books to read over summer vacations and held contests to see who could read the most books. Because of his competitive nature, he worked hard to win these contests, and usually did.

He soon developed a love of reading, and read voraciously, almost nonstop. He loved reading so much that his family always expected him to be the last one ready to leave for an outing because when everyone else was waiting in the car he was usually still sitting in his room reading.

All this reading had its natural effect: Bill learned to read so quickly that he could devour massive quantities of material in a sitting. He also developed the ability to remember almost everything he read.

He read a bit of fiction, but he especially enjoyed nonfiction and reference books, and by the time he was 8-years old, he had read the entire 1960 edition of the World Book Encyclopedia. His reading led him to develop an intense intellectual curiosity that could never be completely satisfied: The more he read, the more he wanted to read. His parents were proud of, and encouraged, his reading by buying him as many books as he wanted.

William and Mary were always supportive of their children. This was also a warm and close family, one which spent much time together talking and playing. There were many lessons the children learned this way, but they were also inspired by their parents' successful careers, advanced education, and obvious work ethics. Plus, their parents did all they could to encouraged the children to strive for excellence. There was no weeknight television. Instead, evenings were typically filled with reading, board games, puzzles, and card games.

It was through these games that Bill acquired his competitiveness, because in his family, no matter what the circumstances, there was always a reward for winning and a penalty for losing. These were just friendly competitions, but to add to the fun, whether a sport or board game, there were always consequences for success and failure.

This ongoing striving for rewards became one of the driving forces in Bill's life. He loved winning these contests and would generally be the one to coordinate the family athletic and board games. Of these games, his favorite was Risk, but he also liked and was good at Monopoly.

Bill's father had a thriving law practice, and Bill's mother was active in various civic and charitable activities. At the dinner table, both parents typically shared what they'd done that day. They discussed their work and volunteer projects and included the children in the conversation. This exposed the children to a variety of activities and concepts and taught them how their parents evaluated situations and made decisions. From this grown-up table-talk, the young boy became adept at dealing with and talking to adults.

Although Mary was busy with lots of social work, she also spent as much time as possible with her children, but when she was not home, her mother, Addle Maxwell, or "Gam" as the children called her, watched them. When the children got home from school, Gam had snacks and activities for them. Like the rest of the family, Gam also loved games, especially bridge, which she enthusiastically taught the children.

Even though Bill's favorite pastime was reading, his parents encouraged him to also try things outside his comfort zone, things he wasn't already good at, such as baseball, football, and soccer.

Bill was indifferent to team sports but inherited his mother's enthusiasm for individual physical activities such as roller-skating, tennis, and snow and water skiing. He also enjoyed hiking with the Boy Scouts, where there was less structure and more freedom to explore.

Even though he considered team sports to be pointless, they still helped give him an early exposure to the power of effective group management and leadership strategies.

When Bill was nine, the family moved to a larger lake-front home in the exclusive Laurelhurst neighborhood of Seattle and Bill started going to Laurelhurst Elementary. But he started to get bored with school and began to only applied himself to subjects that interested him, such as math and reading.

During boring lessons, Bill invented ways of entertaining himself. For example, being left-handed, he would sometimes take notes with his right hand to create a challenge for himself. He also enjoyed looking for incorrectly shelved books in the library. When his teachers noticed this they usually had to force him to go out for recess.

His parents and teachers were worried because Bill wouldn't pay attention in class, his desk was always a mess, and he often made wisecracks or argued with the teachers. He appeared to be a just goof-off and class clown. It was obvious that he had potential, but he was turning into an underachiever.

Bill could learn when he was motivated though. The pastor at the University Congregational Church challenged him to memorize the Sermon on the Mount, a lengthy passage from the Bible and he recited it perfectly, to win a free dinner for himself and his family at the Seattle Space Needle.

Besides his problems at school, by the time he was 11, things were also strained at home. He constantly argued with his parents, and even though he was close to his mother, Bill seemed hardest on her. One time when she asked him what he was doing, he shouted at her, "I'm thinking! Have you ever tried thinking?"

Another time, when he was being particularly nasty to his mother at the dinner table, his exasperated father threw a glass of water in Bill's face. Bill stared at his father and just smirked, "Thanks for the shower."

After a year of increasingly belligerent and rebellious behavior, his parents worried they were losing control of their son and finally took him to a therapist. But the therapist's advice surprised them. He explained that Bill was only trying to claim his independence and advised that they try giving him more leeway, not less.

This strategy helped defuse the situation, but the family also came to realize that Bill had some ideas that couldn't be changed.

His boredom with school continued, but he enjoyed hanging out with an after-school group called the Century Club. It was a group of bright sixth graders who went on field trips, played board games, and held discussions about books and current events. One of the classes Bill enjoyed and did well in was his economics class, where he imagined himself as a young inventor who manufactured and marketed his creations.

When he turned 13, his parents were concerned that he might not be ready for junior high school yet. Intellectually, he was prepared, but he was physically small and shy, his interests were different from those of his peers, and his parents worried that he would have difficulty fitting in. Plus, he was still an inattentive and underachieving student.

His parents concluded that what Bill lacked was focus and challenge. So, although they were firm believers in public education, they decided to transfer him to Seattle's exclusive private preparatory Lakeside School. Here, the class sizes were smaller, and there was more stringent discipline.

His parents weren't disappointed with their decision, and at this new school, their son blossomed in all his classes. He began to thrive not only in math and science but in subjects like drama and English. Bill's turnaround was a huge relief to his parents.

Here is where Bill also met his destiny: At Lakeside School, he discovered computers.

The school thought it would be good if their students became acquainted with computers, but in those days, these machines were larger than refrigerators, and a single one could cost millions. Businesses and universities rented out time on these computer mainframes which received instructions via Teletype machines. Lakeside School raised the funds for student computer use, paying General Electric Company $89 a month for a Teletype and $8 an hour for computer time.

Upon his exposure to computers, Bill experienced a turning point in his life. The convergence of this bright young boy and this promising young technology ignited a spark that helped lead to what would soon become the age of the personal computer.

Bill was amazed by the very concept of computers. The idea of a programmable machine following your instructions was overpowering. He could think of little else. He had found his focus and his challenge.

At Lakeside, Bill's best friend was Kent Evans. Kent had a keen interest in computers, plus in business. The 13-year-old Kent also had plenty of confidence, and confidence was something the shy and bookish Bill Gates wished for himself.

Another close friend at Lakeside was Paul Allen, a student two years older than Bill. Paul shared Bill's fascination with computers, but the two had almost opposite personalities. Paul was quiet and reserved, whereas Bill could sometimes be feisty and combative. They were friends, but they also argued.

The first hurdle was learning how to use the computer. The machine may have fascinated them, but no one — neither teachers nor students — knew anything about it. The only way to learn was by pouring through complex and poorly written computer manuals.

So, that's exactly what Bill and his friends did. They spent all the time they could in the computer lab, reading and teaching themselves programming languages such as BASIC and FORTRAN.

Bill Gates with Paul Allen at Teletype Machine

Eventually, 13-year-old Bill wrote his first computer program, a tic-tac-toe game that the user could play against the computer. He wrote it in the BASIC language he was learning. The program was slow and cumbersome, but it enthralled him that he could enter instructions and the machine would follow them precisely every time.

Seeing how much the other students enjoyed playing his game motivated him to write more programs, and he soon began to imagine all sorts of possibilities. He became obsessed with writing software, and the programs he wrote continued to grow in size and complexity.

His school had initially raised a few thousand dollars to pay for computer time but no one had anticipated the amount of use the machine would get, especially from Bill and a few other zealots. Several students were upset with Bill and complained that he was hogging the computer, but these same students always came to him with their computer questions.

Of course it was true, Bill did hog the computer. He and a few friends even skipped classes to use it, which meant the school's computer fund was soon depleted. The Lakeside Mothers' Club stepped in and raised money with a rummage sale, using their proceeds to buy a Teletype Model 33 ASR terminal and a block of computer time. But even this wasn't enough.

Not long after, another opportunity arose. A new company, Computer Centre Corporation (CCC), had recently opened in Seattle, and because one of their programmers had a child attending Lakeside, the company offered the school a discounted rate for computer time.

But Bill and his friends soon found a better discount. Exploring the new computer, they figured out how to alter the files that recorded how much time was used — so they could get as much free computer time as they wanted. But this hacking led to several computer crashes, and they were eventually caught and banned from the computer for several weeks.

It was this problem of having to pay for computer time that drove Bill to the commercial aspect of computing. Instead of paying others for computer time, he wanted to find a way to get others to pay him to use computers.

Excited by their hacking experience with CCC, Bill Gates, Paul Allen, and two fellow hackers decided to form the Lakeside Programmers Group. They pooled their talents and looked for ways to apply their computer skills in the real world — the real world being one where you make money.

Their first opportunity came from CCC. Impressed with the sophistication of the assaults the students made on their computer, they hired them to find other security weaknesses. In return, the Lakeside Programmers Group had unlimited access to CCC's computer.

The free time they received at C-Cubed, as they called it, got the group seriously into computers. They became hard-core programmers and spent days and nights at CCC's facility. Besides looking for bugs each night, they read all the computer literature left behind by the day shift, and during the day, they'd hang around and pick the brains of anyone who would talk to them. Bill also studied CCC's source code to learn how the back-end of the system worked.

But this arrangement didn't last long. In 1970, after more than a year of financial struggle, CCC went out of business, and the boys lost their free computer time.

Around this time, Bill invented a new way to rebel at school: He had been consistently getting poor grades, but with the fresh cockiness from his C-Cubed adventures, he decided to try for all As; and to do this without taking his books home. He also started skipping math class because he had read the book and felt he didn't need the instruction.

This odd rebellion scheme worked. When aptitude tests were given that year, he placed in the top 10 students nationwide. At this point, he realized he didn't need to rebel any longer. He had nothing to prove. From that time on, he was a straight-A student.

Things also improved at home. Bill was now easier to get along with; however, he still didn't clean his room, which was always a mess of papers, computer tapes, dirty clothes, and reading material. His parents finally gave up and decided to just keep his door closed.

With the loss of C-Cubed, the computer club needed a new source of computer time. The problem was solved when they discovered a few computers could be available to them at the University of Washington, where Paul Allen's father was a librarian.

Bill and Paul soon put these computers to work in a new money-making project. During the summer after 10th grade, Information Sciences Inc (ISI) asked the two boys to write a payroll program. ISI agreed to pay them royalties from the software. This was the first time Bill Gates made money from his computer passion.

Bill's second paid job was for a company that analyzed traffic patterns. The company collected traffic data with pneumatic hoses laid across highways. Time and number of axels were recorded on a punch tape, which was communicated via Teletype to tapes in other locations, where people translated the tapes into information that city planners could use to adjust traffic lights.

Bill and Paul figured they could create software to process the tapes faster and cheaper. They hired classmates to transcribe the punched tapes onto the more modern computer cards. They fed these cards into their program on the University of Washington computers; which printed out charts of traffic flow.

Their next programming opportunity arose at their school. In Bill's junior year, Lakeside merged with Saint Nicholas, an all-girls school. This meant Lakeside now had more than five hundred students, and it was difficult for administrators to manually manage that many student schedules. Each student took eight classes a day; some classes were only once a week, and some included extra lab time.

A few teachers tried writing programs to handle the problem but were unsuccessful. So, they turned to Bill and his friend Kent Evans to create what they called "electronic classroom assignment software." The boys plunged into the project, working day and night, and barely taking time to sleep.

But as they were approaching the completion of this task, tragedy struck. Kent, who enjoyed mountain climbing, was killed in a climbing accident. It was Bill's first experience with death, and he was devastated. He could do nothing for weeks.

After he had time to grieve, and with Paul Allen's help, Bill finished the scheduling program. Plus, he added a tweak to the code, one that would put himself into a class full of the prettiest girls.

Bill and Paul then started a company called Traf-O-Data, with which they planned on producing a system to measure traffic flow and analyze data and eliminate the tedious transcription of the Teletype tape.

But neither Bill nor Paul had any hardware experience. They asked around school until they found another student, Paul Gilbert, who had just this type of expertise.

Since they had no money to pay him, they made Gilbert an equal partner in this enterprise. The project was a tremendous success and grossed the three high schoolers $20,000 ($128,000 in today's dollars).

Bill was elated and wanted to use his earnings to start a full-time company. But his parents had their hearts set on him becoming a lawyer, and they insisted he finish college.

His parents also wanted him to broaden his horizons and spend time doing things that had nothing to do with computers. And so, in 1972, the summer after his junior year, Bill went to Washington, D.C. to work as a congressional page.

With his business successes and his hobnobbing in Washington, Bill was becoming more confident, even starring in three school plays. He was also an aggressive chess and Go player, loved driving about town in the family's red Mustang convertible, and enjoyed waterskiing on the lake. And when he attended his senior prom, he was fully decked out in a white coat, pink ruffled shirt, top hat, and walking stick.

By the time Bill graduated from high school in 1973, he had many options. He scored a perfect 800 on the math portion of his SAT and 790 on the verbal. He won a National Merit Scholarship and was accepted at Harvard, Yale, and Princeton.

Bill chose Harvard and started that fall with every intention of becoming a lawyer.

During his freshman year, he took courses in advanced math, Greek literature, English, social studies, and organic chemistry, but then he frequently skipped these classes and attended others that he preferred just for fun. He also used the university's computers to work on Traf-O-Data.

Bill kept in touch with Paul Allen, who after two years had dropped out of Washington University and moved to Massachusetts to work for Honeywell. Bill and Paul loved working together. As different as they were, they complemented each other's skills. They still had their arguments, but they also answered each other's questions and challenged each other's assumptions.

When he wasn't studying or programming, Bill hung out at a hamburger joint where he could play a new video game called Pong. He got into heated discussions with other students about how computers would soon change the world and average people would have computers in their homes. This was met with scoffs and derision, because, the students asked: why would anyone want anything less than the grand mainframes at the university computer center?

Harvard was an entirely new experience for Bill. For one thing, he found the challenge he wanted. For another though, he was no longer the smartest student and this took some of the wind out of his sails, and he eventually started questioning his purpose at school. He also began to accept that he didn't have a passion for law. He still had a deep desire to succeed, but if not at law, then what? How could he succeed and still follow something he was passionate about?

He briefly considered changing his major to math, then thought it might be better to major in law and science. He even played with the idea of taking a break from college and getting a job, going as far as interviewing with several companies for programming jobs.

During his second year at Harvard, Bill became friends with a math and science student named Steve Balmer. Steve was outgoing and charming and introduced Bill to life beyond studies. The two friends liked playing the video game Breakout and attending all-night poker sessions. Steve's friendship gave Bill a new outlet and a helpful diversion from studying and computers.

In December 1974, a second turning point occurred in Bill's life. It came in the form of a magazine article.

Paul Allen showed Bill Gates the January 1975 edition of Popular Electronics, featuring a story about the Altair 8800 mini-computer kit. On the cover was a mockup of the MITS Altair, the first personal computer. Immediately they grasped its world-changing possibilities and realized this was the personal computing revolution Bill had predicted. "This is it!" said Paul. "It's about to begin!"

The Altair computer kit was made by Micro Instrumentation and Telemetry (MITS), a small company in Albuquerque, New Mexico. Bill and Paul figured the Altair would be powerful enough to run a BASIC interpreter, and they wanted to be the first to offer it. They immediately began developing the software.

Paul Gilbert assembled the computer. Paul Allen created the BASIC program on the Harvard DEC PDP-10 computer that was available for student use. In pencil on yellow legal pads, Bill wrote the assembly language program that would run the Altair's 8-bit 8080 microprocessor which had been released by Intel the previous April. They enlisted the help of another student, Monte Davidoff, to write the math routines.

By March 1975, a preliminary version of the system was complete, and they decided the older-looking Paul Allen should be the one to travel to Albuquerque to demonstrate it to MITS. Once there, it took Allen a full day to get the software running because MITS was still struggling to get their computer working with 7k bytes of memory. But the program worked, and MITS was impressed.

In the April 1975 issue of the Altair Newsletter, the headline read, "Altair BASIC – Up and Running." The software began shipping June 23, 1975, priced at $500.

Paul Allen quit his job at Honeywell to become the MITS Vice President and Director of Software. At first, Bill stayed in school and was listed at the company as "Software Specialist." But to his parents' dismay, he soon dropped out of school to join Paul.

On July 22, 1975, MITS signed a 10-year, exclusive-rights contract with 19-year-old Bill Gates and 21-year-old Paul Allen. They would receive $3,000 at signing and a royalty of between $20 and $60, depending on the version (4K, 8K, or Expanded), for each copy of BASIC sold. The contract had a cap of $180,000 ($800,000 in today's dollars).

In that same month, Bill and Paul formed a partnership. Paul suggested the name, Micro-Soft, a blend of "microcomputer" and "software."

At first, although their BASIC interpreter was hugely popular, they still couldn't make enough money to cover their overhead. The problem was that only about 2 percent of their software was being paid for. Computer enthusiasts preferred to pirate the software, rather than spend $500. To these users, computers were a hobby; they did their programming for free, and they believed others should as well.

Bill Gates disagreed. He thought that passing around free copies was stealing and that he should be paid for his software. In Bill's mind, every success should have a reward.

~~~ SUCCESS ~~~

The phenomenal success of Microsoft turned Bill Gates into the success story of the century. This energetic, argumentative child with a love of reading and an oversized competitive streak, discovered his passion and then pursued it to unprecedented heights.

Although bored with school and headed for mediocrity, he only needed the right challenge to motivate him and awaken him from his apathy. From the encouragement of his early technological successes, this shy class clown soon transformed into a confident straight-A student.

But his success at school was also on his own terms; skipping assigned classes and attending others just for fun. His stubborn independence also meant that his thoughts were also independent and less bound by the limitations of the technology of the time, so he could see beyond these limitations to new possibilities of the future.

Steve Jobs

February 24, 1955 – October 5, 2011

"The people who are crazy enough to think they can change the world, are the ones who do."
— Steve Jobs

On April 1, 1976, Steve Jobs and his friend Steve Wozniak launched Apple Computer with less than $10,000. Apple went public 3 ½ years later, selling 4.6 million shares at $22 each, making Steve an instant billionaire. Now the company is worth more than $750 billion.

Steve Jobs was a passionate and fearless entrepreneur with an exceptionally self-assured personality and a consuming vision to humanize personal electronics. He conquered the music world, the telephone business, and computer-graphic movies, by developing and designing new technological products that people soon loved and made an everyday part of their lives.

Steve Jobs also made computers simpler and more elegant by pioneering such user-friendly innovations as the trash can, windows, drag-and-drop files, and plug-and-play compatibility. And he put music, video, and communications at our fingertips through the creation of iPods, iPads, and iPhones.

The astounding and rapid success of Apple Computer was a reflection of Steve Jobs' keen perception, backed by a commanding personality plus a unique approach to product development, with requirements such as:

- Every production team must build products they would want for themselves.
- Any product that wasn't easy to use was considered worthless to the consumer.
- All products must minimize the decisions required by the user.
- For every product sold, customers must be offered any hand-holding required.

One factor in Steve Jobs' success was his refusal to accept "no" to his proposals and ideas. He called this approach his Reality Distortion Field (RDF), which meant that once he decided that something should happen, he would bend reality to his will until it came true.

The first reality to be bent — which he did as a young boy — was his own personality. Before he changed the world of personal electronics, he changed himself. He made this metamorphosis from a shy, socially awkward boy, into an ambitious, irrepressible technological leader, by seeking role models he admired and persistently striving to emulate them.

~~~

Thursday, February 24, 1955

About 40 babies were born that day in San Francisco, but this one wouldn't be going home with his mother. His mother had arranged to give him up for adoption. In 1955, adoption was still the standard practice for avoiding the stigma of single parenthood.

In the middle of the night, the doctor phoned the new would-be parents; a lawyer and his wife, but the couple had changed their minds, and now only wanted a girl. The doctor called the next couple on his list, Paul and Clara Jobs, who accepted immediately, and the baby became Stephen Paul Jobs.

Steve's new parents had met nine years earlier. At the end of World War II, in March 1946, Paul Reinhold Jobs was discharged from the Coast Guard and stepped off his ship into San Francisco. Two days later, he met Clara Hagopian. Ten days after meeting, they were engaged. He was 23, and she was 21. Both were anxious to put the weight of the war behind them and to settle into a peaceful life and raise a family.

Paul was a tattooed engine mechanic, six feet tall, with a resemblance to James Dean. He grew up on a dairy farm in Germantown, Wisconsin. His father was an abusive alcoholic, but fortunately Paul developed a gentle disposition which he usually tried to conceal beneath a rough exterior.

Paul dropped out of high school and spent several years wandering the Midwest and working temporary jobs as a mechanic. After Pearl Harbor, 19-year-old Paul joined the Coast Guard and spent the war ferrying troops to Patton's army.

Clara was the daughter of Armenian refugees living in New Jersey. When Clara was a toddler, her family moved to the Mission District in San Francisco. Clara was a sweet, shy young woman, with slightly dark skin and warm brown hair, and was working as a bookkeeper when she met Paul.

When Paul and Clara married, they had little money and spent the first few years living with Paul's parents in Wisconsin. They then moved to Indiana where Paul found a job working as a machinist at International Harvester. Paul supplemented his income by buying, repairing, and selling cars. He could buy a car in the junkyard for $50 and usually get around $250 when he was done with it. His knowledge of cars eventually led Paul to quit his machinist job and become a full-time used car salesman.

After a while, Clara began missing her hometown, so in 1952, the couple moved to San Francisco, where Paul took a job of repossessing cars.

The couple wanted children, but nine years into their marriage they'd still had no success. So, at 32 and 30 years old, they decided to adopt.

Clara had an earlier marriage which she rarely discussed. Her first husband died in the war soon after they were married, but during that marriage, Clara suffered an ectopic pregnancy, which might explain why she was unable to get pregnant again.

Steve's birth mother, 23-year-old, Joanne Schieble, was of German heritage and grew up in the rural outskirts of Green Bay, Wisconsin. The birth father, 23-year-old, Abdulfattah "John" Jandali, was the youngest of nine children in a prominent Syrian family. His father owned several successful businesses and oil refineries.

Joanne and John were enrolled at the University of Wisconsin, and both their families put a premium on education. But Joanne's father was Catholic and threatened to disown his daughter if she married John, who was a Muslim.

When Joanne got pregnant, she was afraid to tell her father, and so she decided to put her baby up for adoption. Her only stipulation was that the baby must be adopted by college graduates. When she discovered that the baby was placed with Paul and Clara Jobs, a high school dropout and a clerical worker, she only agreed to sign the adoption papers after Paul and Clara made a written promise to give their son a college education.

At first, the couple and their new baby lived in a small apartment in San Francisco's foggy Sunset district. After three months, they rented an inexpensive house in an industrial area in the southern part of the city.

Two years later, the family adopted a second child, a baby girl named Patty.

Steve was a curious and energetic toddler, with a habit of waking up at 4 in the morning. His parents bought him a rocking horse, hoping it would keep him quiet until they woke up. This wasn't always successful since his room also included a phonograph player and a stack of Little Richards records.

His curiosity and hyperactivity made Steve a handful. His parents once rushed him to the hospital with burns on his hands after he stuck a bobby pin in an electrical outlet. Another time, they dashed to the hospital to have his stomach pumped after he ate a bottle of ant poison.

This was evidently the type of child who needed plenty of supervision but fortunately like most mothers in the 1950s, Clara stayed home with her children. She watched Steve play and prepared him for school by teaching him to read.

When Steve was five, the family moved again, this time buying a small three-bedroom house in Mountain View, a developing suburban area south of San Francisco.

Paul spent a good deal of time with his son whenever he could. The two worked together on projects in Paul's immaculately organized garage. When Steve was five, his father set him up with his own sectioned-off portion of the workbench.

Steve was impressed with his father's craftsmanship and attention to detail. He considered his dad to be a genius with his hands, someone who could take apart and repair anything. Paul taught Steve the importance of quality and pride of workmanship. He stressed that all parts of a project should be well-made with precision and care, including the parts no one will see.

When Steve started school, he had difficulty adjusting. At Monta Loma Elementary, he enjoyed reading and chasing butterflies at recess. But he was uninterested in the rest, and he didn't respond well to the controlled, structured environment that school imposed. Plus, he was shy and a bit of a loner, and would storm off and cry when he didn't get his way.

He may also have had some concerns about being adopted. Although Paul and Clara were always open with him about his adoption, he may not have been clear on what adoption meant.

One day, when he was seven, he told the girl across the street that he was adopted. "So, does that mean your real parents didn't want you?" she asked. He hadn't thought about this before, and he ran into the house crying. His parents said he was definitely wanted and told him, "We specifically picked you out."

At school, Steve continued to struggle. By the third grade, he'd pretty much decided school was a waste of time. Instead of doing classwork, he and his buddy Rick Ferrentino upset their class with pranks, like releasing a snake in the classroom or setting off firecrackers under the teacher's desk.

The next year, the principal decided to separate these two boys and as a result, Steve was assigned to Mrs. Imogene "Teddy" Hill, who taught an advanced fourth-grade class. This was a teacher unlike any Steve had previously encountered and became an important turning point in his life.

Mrs. Hill recognized that Steve was bored and so she offered him a challenge. She told him that if he took a math workbook home, completed it, and got 80 percent correct, she'd reward him with a lollipop and $5. He not only succeeded, but began developing such respect for this teacher, that he worked hard to excel in her class so he could continue to impress her.

At the end of the year, Mrs. Hill had Steve tested, and he scored at the high school sophomore level. She suggested he skip the next two years, but his parents, who were more familiar with their son's maturity level, agreed to him only skipping one year.

This was 1963, and the booming Kennedy economy and flourishing high-tech industry continued to expand their new suburb. After watching the success a neighbor was having, Paul Jobs decided to get a real estate license and switch careers to selling houses. Although this venture went well the first year, by the second, it was evident that Paul's rough manner wasn't suited for a people-oriented business.

The family's income suffered, and this change was confusing to young Steve. He could see neighbors enjoying all the new gadgets coming on the market, but his family was stuck on a tight budget. One day, when his teacher asked the class if they had any questions they didn't understand about the universe, Steve responded that he didn't understand why all of a sudden, his dad was so broke.

To dig himself out of this financial hole: Paul went back to work as a machinist, Clara took a part-time job in the payroll department of a local company, and they took out a second mortgage on their home. Paul also continued adding to his income by restoring junk cars.

Steve watched his father work but wasn't interested in mechanical things or getting his hands dirty. He became more interested when his father explained the rudiments of automotive electrical systems, which became Steve's first exposure to electronics. More interesting were trips with his father to scavenge junkyards for parts. Here, he was impressed with his father's uncanny knowledge of prices and excellent bargaining skills.

Paul may not have been successful in real estate, but more homes continued to be built and sold around them, and more and more technology workers moved into the area.

Following the successful Soviet launch of Sputnik in 1957, the U.S. poured millions of dollars into technology catch-up; and a lot of this money found its way to Palo Alto, home of the high-tech Hewlett-Packard company. The existence of HP made this a good place to look for the kind of talent required for similar businesses that were starting up.

By 1965, the Palo Alto area was becoming a hotbed of technology. Besides Hewlett Packard, there were other high-tech companies, including Fairchild Semiconductor, Westinghouse, Lockheed Missiles and Space Division, and the NASA Ames Research Center. Palo Alto was an exciting place for engineers to live, and neighborhood conversations were typically focused on the latest electronics developments.

And these advancements were accelerating. This was the year that Gordon Moore, founder of Integrated Electronics Corporation (soon abbreviated to Intel), drew a graph of the increasing speeds of integrated circuits, demonstrating a doubling every two years, an observation that became known as Moore's Law.

Steve and his friends were surrounded by electronics engineers, electronic components and tools, and daily news of electronic progress. The most exciting developments were in the field of computers.

Steve saw his first computer when he was 10 years old, when in the summer of 1965, his father took him to visit the local NASA Ames Research Center. Before this, Steve had only seen computers in the movies, and these were mostly images of whirling tape drives and flashing lights. It was a special privilege to see a real computer, and Steve was captivated by it. He was allowed to type instructions into the Teletype machine and watched the computer go tk ... tk ... tk ... while it executed his instructions, until the noise stopped, and out of the printer came his results.

NASA Ames Research Center

That fall, Steve had to switch to a new school. Since he was skipping fifth grade, he would have to be enrolled in the Crittenden Middle School. Crittenden was only eight blocks from his elementary school, but it was a completely different environment, full of ethnic gangs. It wasn't unusual for these kids to bring knives to school, and every day there were fights and shakedowns in the bathrooms. Being socially awkward and a year younger than his classmates, added to his chances of being bullied at this school.

By the middle of seventh grade, Steve gave his parents an ultimatum. He refused to go back to school unless it was to a different school.

Money was tight for the family, but somehow, they scraped together enough for a down payment on a $21,000 house at 2066 Crist Drive, three miles south, in the flatlands of Los Altos. It was a one-story house with three bedrooms and an attached garage that the father and son could share as a workshop.

Most importantly, the house was just inside the Cupertino-Sunnyvale School District, which was considered one of the best and safest in the valley.

This was a stereotypical mid-century suburb. The houses were modeled on ones built by the real estate developer Joseph Eichler and were intended for a mass-market. Steve was impressed with the home's clean, elegant design, and smart features, such as the radiant floor heating.

It was an exciting and beautiful place to live; with apricot and plum orchards, clear open skies, and a booming economy based on the modern technology being developed by the local engineers.

Their new neighborhood had an even higher concentration of electronic engineering families, and possibly the highest concentration of scientifically oriented people anywhere in one town. Each block had at least a half-dozen garage workshops.

Seven doors from Steve's house, an HP engineer named Larry Lang spent a great deal of time working on projects in his garage, and enjoyed showing what he was building to the neighborhood kids. Larry was a ham radio operator and a hard-core electronics guy. Steve liked hanging out at Larry's garage, and Larry liked teaching the curious boy about electronics.

To help Steve learn, Larry introduced him to Heath kits. These were electronic kits with color-coded parts and manuals that described the concepts of what was being built. Paul bought several of these kits for his son. Not only did Steve learn about electronics, but it was also a tremendous boost to his confidence to discover he could build complicated real-world things on his own.

Larry also got Steve involved in the Hewlett-Packard Explorers Club, where students assembled in the company's cafeteria on Tuesday nights to hear engineers talk about projects they were working on.

Between Larry Lang and the Explorer's club, a whole new world was opening to Steve. His father had exposed him to mechanical things, but the things Steve learned from Larry were on a whole new level.

Steve noticed that these were things his father didn't usually understand, and this got Steve thinking that maybe he was smarter than his parents. At first, he felt shame for thinking this, but it was an unforgettable childhood moment. This idea, along with the fact that he was adopted, made him feel detached and separate not only from his parents, but from other people as well. He was also convinced that his parents knew he was special and were willing to do anything to accommodate his uniqueness.

Plenty of boys in the neighborhood shared his interest in electronics. He developed a friendship with a boy named Bill Fernandez, a slight, intense child, in the same grade, and a year older than Steve. These two boys had more than electronics in common; both were skinny, scrawny, relatively uncoordinated, and outsiders at school.

In ninth grade, Steve started at Homestead High School. He didn't have many friends his age but started hanging out with some of the seniors. The older boys shared his interest in math and electronics, but many were also getting into the new counter-culture of the late '60s.

It was at this time that Steve got his first view of the two antithetical worlds that were evolving in American society. On one side, there was Conservatism, Republicanism, patriotism, and the thoroughly tame ditty "Up, Up and Away" by the Fifth Dimension, which won the Grammy's Best Song of the Year award. On the other side, there was the Vietnam anti-war protests at Berkley, the Summer of Love in San Francisco; and the progressive music of Sergeant Pepper's Lonely Hearts Club Band.

But the protests and hippies were still worlds away from Steve's neighborhood, where excitement came from electronics, technology, and computers.

At 12 years old, Steve saw his first desktop computer. Most computers then were huge, generally the size of refrigerators or whole rooms. The Explorers Club showed the students a Hewlett-Packard 9100A, which weighed 40 pounds and was about the size of a suitcase. It had its own cathode-ray tube display, and was totally self-contained — no wires leading to a computer in another room. This was the first desktop scientific calculator, and in 1968 it was advertised as a "personal computer," and the lucky kids in the Explorers Club were allowed to play with it.

Steve fell in love with this machine. It could be programmed in BASIC or APL, and every day, he hitched a ride to the Hewlett-Packard research lab and tried to write programs for it.

Paul was now working at Spectra-Physics, in nearby Santa Clara, where they made lasers for electronic and medical products. Steve was fascinated by the extreme precision needed to produce these devices, and with parts he scrounged or were brought home by his father, he built his own laser as a school project.

Kids at the Explorers Club were also encouraged to build projects, and Steve decided to build a frequency counter, a device which measures pulses per second. He needed some parts that HP made, so he looked up the company CEO in the phone book (this was before unlisted numbers) and called him at home. Bill Hewlett answered the phone and spoke with Steve for twenty minutes. Steve not only got the parts but was also offered a job in the plant that made frequency counters. So, for the summer after ninth grade, 14-year-old Steve had his first job, working on an HP assembly line "putting nuts and bolts on things."

He learned two important lessons that summer. For one, he experienced the power and independent feeling of having a job and earning an income. But he also was able to witness the inner workings and management style of this almost mythical company.

HP started with Bill Hewlett and David Packard working in David's garage designing control devices for animation cameras, for which Walt Disney was one of their first clients. They later started creating small computer systems. The company became well-known for excellent engineering and high-quality products, which made it the place every engineer wanted to work.

Hewlett-Packard was a unique company with a reputation for "doing it right," regardless of cost. The company offered employees flexible work hours, spacious offices, guaranteed lifetime employment, and beautifully landscaped environments. HP attracted many of the best engineers and technicians to the area. It was a company ahead of its time and a favorite subject in the media and among the electronic hobbyists in the area, including Steve and his friends.

One day, his friend Bill Fernandez told Steve that he was working with a neighbor to build a computer in his garage. This neighbor was Steve Wozniak, a boy a few years older who lived across the street from Bill. Although the older boy had already graduated from high school, "Woz" as he was known, was still an electronics legend at the school. Building a computer had been a dream of his for some time, and now in this partnership with Bill, he was about to build his first one. Woz did the designing, and Bill did the assembling in his organized and well-equipped garage.

Bill brought Steve to meet Woz and to see their nearly-completed machine. Bill also figured Steve and Woz might hit it off because they shared an interest in electronics and both seemed fond of pranks.

Steve was impressed with the machine, even though it looked like nothing more than a box with rows of lights and switches. He was also glad to meet this guy who supposedly knew so much about electronics.

Woz recommended to Bill and Steve that they should enroll in McCollum's electronics class, and the two agreed to take it together.

John McCollum had a flair for dramatic demonstrations, such as wild lightning sparks flashing from a Tesla coil. He also mixed the theoretical underpinnings of electronics with a product-oriented approach, to develop practical engineers who knew how to actually make things.

But Steve wasn't excited about the course. This may partly be from his dislike of the teacher's disciplinary attitude — McCollum was a no-nonsense ex-Navy fighter pilot who allowed no one to question his authority. But Steve also seemed to be getting bored with the design and theoretical aspects of electronics. He quit the three-year electronics course after the first year.

The summer after 10th grade, Steve worked again at HP, and when school started, he took a weekend job at Haltek, a block-long junkyard of electronic components. Haltek was where garage designers went for parts. Here, he developed a good understanding of components and prices and used this knowledge at the San Jose Swap Meet, to haggle for components in order to sell them for a profit to his boss at Haltek.

Now that he had some money (and with a little financial assistance from his dad), Steve bought his first car, a tiny red Fiat 850 coupe. It wasn't reliable, but it fulfilled that all-important need of teenage boys: freedom.

In the beginning of the new decade, his hometown was suddenly getting national attention. The January 1971 edition of Electronic News launched a series called "Silicon Valley USA," and suddenly, the Santa Clara Valley had a new name and identity.

That year, Bill, Woz, and Steve spent much of their time together, working on and discussing their various projects. Woz turned Steve onto Bob Dylan, and they collected as much pirated Dylan music as they could find. The two became close friends and when Wozniak enrolled in Berkeley, Steve drove 40 miles two or three times a week to visit him.

One Sunday afternoon in September 1971, Wozniak read an article in Esquire magazine describing how hackers could make long-distance phone calls for free by replicating the tones that routed signals on the AT&T network.

Woz immediately called Steve to read parts of the article to him. The hackers' tone generators were called Blue Boxes. These tone generators were analog, which means they weren't reliable and couldn't always generate a stable enough tone.

By late November, Wozniak succeeded in creating the first digital Blue Box using diodes and transistors from Radio Shack. The device was about the size of two packs of playing cards. The first thing Woz and Steve put it to use on was making long-distance prank calls.

One call was to the Vatican. In the middle of the night, Woz told the person who answered that he was Henry Kissinger. This person started waking up cardinals in the hierarchy, and finally, they sent someone to wake up the Pope. But when the boys started giggling and then burst out laughing, the Vatican realized this wasn't really the Secretary of State.

The boys eventually tired of their prank calls but Steve remained inspired by the magic that for a few hundred dollars they could build a tiny thing (the box), which could control a giant thing (the world-wide telephone network) from their home in Cupertino. They were struck with a sense of power when they realized that they were controlling billions of dollars of infrastructure.

Steve suggested that perhaps this could be a business and they began building their digital Blue Boxes for $40 and selling them to other students for $150. This was the beginning of a relationship that continued throughout their partnership in Apple Computer: Wozniak imagined neat inventions, and Steve figured out how to make them user-friendly, package them, and sell them for a profit.

In spring of 1972, Steve met his first real girlfriend. Chrisann Brennan was an attractive girl with light brown hair, green eyes, and high cheekbones, and was enduring the break-up of her parents. By summer, Steve decided that he and Chrisann would move to a cabin in the hills above Los Altos. His father said, "over my dead body," but Steve simply said good-bye and walked out.

At the cabin, Chrisann painted, while Steve wrote poetry and played guitar. True to the hippy lifestyle, they were always broke. So, when Steve lost his Fiat to an engine fire, he had to take a $3-an-hour promotional job at the Westgate Shopping Center in San Jose where he was required to dress in a full-body costume as Alice in Wonderland. Woz and Chrisann joined him, Woz as the Mad Hatter, and Chrisann as the White Rabbit. Steve was determined to earn enough for another car but he hated the job and had to restrain himself from smacking some of the children.

Meanwhile, his parents were begging him to return to school to honor the promise they'd made that he would have a college education. Steve responded passive-aggressively, insisting he would only go to Reed College, a private, and expensive, liberal arts school in Portland, Oregon.

When his parents relented and in September 1972 drove him to the school, he refused to let them on campus and left the car without saying goodbye. He wanted to look like he'd just arrived out of nowhere, a free spirit with no roots and no background.

A week later, Steve met Daniel Kottke, a long-hair, bearded student from a wealthy New York family. They shared an interest in Zen and Dylan, and Steve was attracted to Daniel's flower-child demeanor. Although Daniel expressed disdain for material possessions, he was impressed with Steve's TEAC recorder and collection of Dylan bootlegs.

Steve, Daniel, and Daniel's girlfriend, Elizabeth Holmes, attended love festivals at the Hare Krishna temple, went for free vegetarian meals at the Zen center, and occasionally hitchhiked to the coast together.

Steve took Zen seriously. He was attracted to its minimalist aesthetics and preferred its intuitive decision making over the more common: logical, analytical approach. But given his intense nature, he found it difficult to achieve the promised inner peace. However, he still assumed the trappings of the day: He grew his hair long, went barefoot (or wore sandals in the winter), and experimented with one exotic diet after another.

A few months after starting at Reed College, Steve met Robert Friedland, Reed's student body president, and son of a prosperous Chicago architect. Steve was trying to raise spending money by selling his IBM Selectric typewriter to Robert. Robert was four years older than Steve and had recently completed a one-year prison sentence for possession of $125,000 worth of LSD. Steve thought he was far-out and was instantly mesmerized by him.

At first the two were opposites, but Steve soon learned to copy much of Robert's behavior and mannerisms. He honed Robert's trick of using silent stares to control people, and he absorbed his techniques to make himself the center of attention. He also learned to shed his shyness, take charge of situations, and capture attention when he entered a room. These were useful and effective skills Steve would apply throughout his career.

During the summer, Friedland was caretaking a neglected 220-acre apple farm that belonged to a rich, eclectic uncle. He turned it into a commune, calling it the All One Farm. Steve worked there for free and led a group of hippies who also worked for free, pruning orchards and chopping firewood.

Steve left the farm when it finally dawned on him that Robert was the only one making money off the venture. He realized his guru was a charlatan, however Steve remained friends with Robert because he appreciated the fact that Robert was a very effective charlatan.

Steve was definitely more interested in lessons he could learn from Robert than from school. He still enjoyed going to the prestigious Reed College, but he was bored with his classes and rarely went to them. The few classes he attended, like dance class to meet girls, were classes he wasn't even enrolled in.

His parents had saved all their lives for Steve's college education, but he had lost interest in it. In fact, he had no idea what he wanted to do with his life. So, just as when he got bored in 3rd grade or bored in Mr. McCollum's electronics class, he quit Reed College.

But regardless of the fact he'd officially dropped out, he continued to hang out at the school for the next 18 months, attending the occasional class when he was interested. One of these was a calligraphy class, where he learned about typefaces and letter spacing. In this class, he was fascinated by the subtle ways that fonts could affect a message.

By the end of 1973, Steve was living in an unheated garage apartment for $20 a month and occasionally worked at a job maintaining some of the school's electronic equipment. Chrisann visited him once in a while, but he had a tendency to be cold and rude to her, and this relationship eventually sputtered to an end.

In February 1974, Steve moved back in with his parents. Robert Friedland was in India, seeking spiritual re-awakening, and Steve needed to earn money so he could join him.

He found a classified ad in the San Jose Mercury that said, "Have fun, make money." That day he walked into the lobby of Atari and announced he wouldn't leave until they gave him a job.

The personnel director was startled by Steve's unkempt hair, dirty clothes, and sandals. He was also put off by his smell, which was possibly a result of his current fruit-and-vegetable diet. The director called the chief engineer, Al Alcorn, and said, "We've got a hippie kid in the lobby. He says he's not leaving until we hire him. Should we call the cops or let him in?"

For some reason, Al decided to give the kid a try and hired him as a technician for $5 an hour. Steve was to report to a straitlaced engineer named Don Lang. On Steve's first day, Lang called Alcorn, "This guy's a goddam hippie with B.O. and he's impossible to work with! Why did you do this to me?"

But Steve had found his calling. Although he later managed to make a short visit to India, he'd now discovered a new passion. He'd seen his first computer at 10 years old, did BASIC programming when he was 12. At 14 he'd watched his friend Bill Fernandez build a computer in his garage and Steve Wozniak program it. But now, at 19, he had a real computer job, on the night shift because of his smell.

Atari was a video game manufacturer, and at that time it had fewer than 50 employees. Their hit product was Pong, the first (and incredibly successful) video game console. It was a simple game of hitting a block of pixels back and forth by controlling digital paddles with knobs. Steve was drawn to the sheer simplicity of the game.

Not only was the product appealing, but so was the company's founder and CEO, Nolan Bushnell. Bushnell was a burly visionary, and an entrepreneur with a charismatic showmanship personality that seemed crazy enough to change the world — another role model for Steve to emulate.

~~~ VISIONARY ~~~

Steve Jobs was a visionary who not only changed the personal electronics business, but also the way in which other companies approached design and marketing: Instead of developing a technology and then looking for customers to sell their new product to, instead he started with the customer's desired experience and worked backwards to develop a suitable technology.

Who could have predicted that this hyperactive, accident-prone child who cried when he didn't get his way, and quit whenever he got bored; would someday create the kind of products people would stand in line to buy?

With a spark of motivation from a caring teacher plus a commitment to reconstructing his personality in the image of those he admired, this formerly shy loner accumulated a series of successes which developed into a new and powerful attitude of supreme confidence.

With his new confidence and forceful personality, and unwillingness to accept "no," Steve Jobs pursued his own unrelenting focus to envision, build, and promote completely new marvels that previously had only existed in the world of science fiction.

Walt Disney

December 5, 1901 – December 15, 1966

"It's kind of fun to do the impossible."
— Walt Disney

Imagine a world without Disney cartoons, movies, or Disneyland. Most people would agree — especially children — that it would be a world with less happiness.

Walt Disney sprinkled bits of happiness into millions of lives with an array of imaginative entertainment productions, including:

- Mickey Mouse
- Pluto
- Goofy
- Donald Duck
- Snow White
- Pinocchio
- The Sorcerer's Apprentice
- Fantasia

- Dumbo
- Bambi
- Cinderella
- Alice In Wonderland
- Lady and the Tramp
- 20,000 Leagues Under the Sea
- The Mickey Mouse Club

...and of course, the "happiest place on Earth," Disneyland.

Walt Disney was a dreamer with the courage and persistence to make his dreams come true, turning them into entirely new industries.

This small-town farm boy, bored with school and in love with drawing, turned his childhood passion into an entertainment and media conglomerate.

Through his art and imagination, Disney became an international symbol of entertainment and delight and is recognized as one of the most creative people in the world, receiving 248 awards, including a record-breaking 22 Oscars.

Today the Walt Disney company encompasses a multitude of venues, including movie studios, cruise lines, vacation resorts, children's books, magazines, the ABC network, plus a worldwide chain of magical theme parks.

All of Disney's enchanting creations started with a boy who had dream of doing animation and owning his own studio.

~~~

Thursday, December 5, 1901

At 35 minutes after midnight, in an upstairs bedroom of a small house at 1249 Tripp Avenue, on Chicago's West Side, Walter Elias Disney was born to Flora and Elias Charles Disney. The baby was fine-featured and golden-haired, soft-looking like his mother's side of the family, without the thin hard features of his father's.

Elias Disney and Flora Call had married 14 years earlier in 1888 on New Year's Day. She was 19, and he was 29. They were married in Flora's home in Kismet, Florida, 50 miles north of where Walt Disney World would eventually be built.

Elias, the eldest of 10 children, descended from Irish immigrants and grew up on a backwoods farm in southwestern Ontario, Canada. When he was 19, his family moved to Ellis County, Kansas, where his father, Kepple Disney, purchased 300 acres.

Seven years later, the Disneys moved again, this time to escape the howling wilderness and brutal Kansas winters. They and a neighboring farm family, the Calls, moved to Lake County, Florida, this time to try citrus farming.

Both families came from a heritage of restlessness and aspirations. Whether pursuing dreams of gold mines, oil wells, or salt wells, their family trees were filled with ancestors who farmed only when they couldn't find other opportunities to chase.

Elias was a stern and devoutly religious man who valued frugality, honesty, and hard work. He had a thin taut body, blue eyes, copper-colored hair, and sunken cheeks. It was a pioneer's face — the face of American Gothic. He was also a man who kept his emotions in check — except for anger, which was more difficult for him to control.

Flora grew up in Ellis, Kansas, in a family of 10 children. Flora was of English descent with ancestors who'd arrived in America in 1636. In her early teens, she was sent to school to become a teacher. Flora was a sweet and amiable girl, with a spark of mischievousness, which offset Elias's intense seriousness.

Elias and Flora spent their first two years of marriage on the family farm in Florida, but in the spring of 1890, after a citrus crop failure and the accidental death of Flora's father, the couple moved to Chicago. Elias worked as a carpenter for the upcoming Chicago World's Fair, and later took a job building homes for $7 a week. Working together, the couple also built their own two-story wooden cottage where Walt was born.

Walt had three older brothers: Herbert, Raymond, and Roy. The closest to his age, Roy, was eight years his senior. His sister Ruth was born two years after him.

Much of Elias and Flora's life revolved around their local church, where Elias served as a deacon, played the fiddle at services, and delivered sermons when the minister was absent, and where Flora served as church treasurer. Walt was even named after their minister, Walter Parr, who baptized him a year later at the Saint Paul's Congregational Church.

It was a rough neighborhood though, and just after Walt turned four, an incident occurred that convinced the family to move: Two boys from their church shot and killed a policeman during an attempted robbery. Elias and Flora wanted a better environment for their children, so they decided to return to farming.

In February 1906, they sold their house for $1,800, and in March they bought a 40-acre farm, 400 miles southwest of Chicago in a remote area of Missouri for $3,000. In April they added another five acres for $400. The farm included a one-story house with whitewashed siding and green trim, and it was located just a quarter mile from the small town of Marceline.

Elias and his two oldest sons drove out first by wagon to prepare the farm. Young Walt, his mother, his brother Roy, and his baby sister Ruth followed soon by rail. When the Atchison, Topeka and Santa Fe Railway train pulled into Marceline, the family was greeted by M. A. Coffman, one of their new neighbors, waving to them from his wagon parked next to a grain elevator.

They climbed onto Coffman's wagon, and he drove them to their new home. Walt was dazzled by the farmhouse. The first thing he noticed was the park-like front yard with its carpet of green grass and crowd of weeping willows.

The farm wasn't large, but to Walt it was perfect. There were foxes, rabbits, squirrels, opossums, and raccoons; and the farm included orchards, livestock, and row crops. Five acres were planted in apple, peach, and plum trees, as well as grapevines and berry plants. The house was surrounded by orange trees, silver maples, cedars, dogwoods, and lilacs. There was also a hog pen, chickens, milk cows, and horses. To a city kid from crowded, smoky Chicago, it was heaven.

Walt was also delighted by the quaint town of Marceline. East of the Locus River off Highway 5, and with the Santa Fe Railway tracks running diagonally through its center, it was exactly how the young boy imagined a small town should look.

Marceline, Missouri

Marceline was home to about 4,500 residents, with many elegant houses and beautiful lawns. Kansas Avenue, in the center of town, was unpaved but included all the necessary shops: a dry goods store, a meat market, a creamery, and a three-level department store. The town also had a tavern, ice store, hardware store, jewelry store, a two-story hotel; and on one corner stood a free-standing clock. In the center of town was

Ripley Square, a beautifully wooded park with a band gazebo, a pond, and an old cannon sitting next to a mound of cannonballs.

In time, the town's greatest impact on Walt wasn't just its appearance, but its generous spirit of community. People cared for and were tolerant of one another, and they pulled together to manage the many building and repair projects of rural life.

Living on the farm imbued Walt with an affection for animals. He and his brothers liked to ride together on an old horse named Charley. They also enjoyed herding the pigs, sometimes even riding on their backs. And wherever Walt went, his frisky Maltese terrier followed.

In the summer, the boys fished and went skinny-dipping in the Yellow Creek near the house. In winter, they sledded, and when the creek was frozen, they skated and afterwards built a bonfire on the shore to warm themselves.

There was also a steady stream of entertainment that came through town. It was in Marceline that 5-year-old Walt saw his first circus, which inspired him to produce his own "Disney Circus" in the family barn. He charged 10 cents admission and put on a show with animals that he dressed in clothing.

Walt visited Buffalo Bill's Wild West Show when it stopped in town. He also attended all the traveling tent shows, which included speakers, musicians, entertainers, and preachers.

A theatrical group toured Marceline when Walt was 6, and he broke open his piggy bank to purchase admission to Maude Adams' presentation of Peter Pan. He was impressed and later played the title role in his school production of the play, while his brother Roy operated the hoist that enabled Walt to fly.

Walt also saw his first motion picture in Marceline: *A Life of Christ.* He took his little sister and received a scolding when they returned home after dark.

For Walt, farm life and small-town living were what dreams were made of. These indeed were his halcyon days.

But farm life was also cramped. The back parlor of their farmhouse was converted into a bedroom for Herbert and Ray, and Walt and Roy had to share a bed. As a result, regardless of their 8-year age difference, the brothers grew very close during many late-night conversations they shared in their tiny bedroom.

As crowded as their farmhouse was, the Disneys always had room for visitors. Grandma Disney, Elias's widowed mother, sometimes took the train from Ellis to visit the family. It was great fun for Walt to watch her tease and bedevil his straitlaced father. Once while out walking with Walt, she had the boy crawl under a neighbor's fence to fetch some turnips. Elias was mortified when he discovered their transgression, which made the incident all the more entertaining for Walt.

Walt also enjoyed visits from his Uncle Mike Martin, husband of Flora's older sister Alice. He was a conductor on the train that ran between Marceline and Fort Madison, Iowa. Uncle Mike walked or hitchhiked from the station to the farm, many times carrying brightly striped bags of candy for the children.

Walt marveled at the grand and magnificent trains that rumbled into town and felt special to have an uncle who worked on one. These trains were an essential part of everyday life, delivering supplies and connecting far-flung relatives. Walt's biggest thrill was when his family took the train and Uncle Mike let him ride up front in the cab.

Walt's favorite visitor was Uncle Edmund Disney. At the time, when a person was slow or apparently of limited intelligence, people were less prone to seek a medical diagnosis or name for the condition, and the Disney family simply considered that Edmund was "retarded." When Edmund showed up, it was always a welcome surprise. He would just suddenly walk in the door and announce, "I'm here."

Walt loved playing with him because Uncle Ed seemed never to grow up. He was a role model for the boy because he had zero inhibitions and did everything he wanted to do. But many times, his visits were quite brief because he would just as suddenly leave to visit someone else.

When he was ready to go, he would walk to the railroad tracks, flag down a train, and say, "I want a ride," then hop on and be gone.

Uncle Robert Disney lived a mile to the west. He owned a larger farm of 440 acres and was probably the person who convinced Elias to move to the area. Uncle Robert was the opposite of Uncle Ed. He was rich and somewhat pretentious, and he wore ostentatious clothes and drove a flashy wagon. The family loved him, but behind his back, the neighbors referred to him as "Uncle Gold Bug."

Uncle Robert's wife, Aunt Margaret, oftentimes brought Walt a gift of Big Chief drawing tablets and pencils, which to her nephew were treasured possessions. Aunt Margaret, the only aunt Walt called "auntie," adored his drawings and regarded her nephew as a boy wonder.

Walt loved to draw from the time he could hold a pencil. One day, he used some tar he found in a barrel to paint several childish depictions of animals on the side of their whitewashed house. Unexpectedly to the young boy, the drawings wouldn't wash off; to his parents' dismay, they became permanent decorations to their home.

Walt also liked tagging along with a neighbor, Doc Sherwood, a retired medical doctor with the time and patience to share his knowledge and wisdom with the boy. He spent so much time with Doc Sherwood that he was almost an adopted son. Because the boy was inquisitive and asked so many questions, Doc Sherwood once gave him what turned into a lasting piece of advice when he said, "Don't ever be afraid to admit your ignorance."

One day, Doc Sherwood offered Walt a nickel to draw a picture of his horse. The subject had difficulty staying still, so the result looked more like a jumble of legs than a horse. But this crayon scribble became the first time Walt was paid for his art.

Farm life may have been excellent for the children, but unfortunately, Elias didn't have much aptitude for farming. He once told a neighbor that he didn't believe in fertilizing his fields because it was like "giving whiskey to a man — he felt better for a while, but then was worse off than before." His crops never did well, and Elias began doing carpentry for neighbors to make ends meet.

Things got worse in the fall of 1907, when Elias and his two oldest sons had a serious argument, eventually ending in the boys leaving home. Herbert and Ray sold some wheat Uncle Robert had let them grow on his land, and when Elias heard of this, he insisted that if they were living under his roof, the money must go toward paying off the farm.

Herbert and Ray had had enough. They didn't like working on the farm for free, and now they couldn't keep the money they'd earned outside the farm. In the spring of the next year, at 19 and 17 years old, they moved back to Chicago, where Uncle Robert helped them get jobs as bank clerks.

Without Herbert and Ray, Elias only had 14-year-old Roy and 6-year-old Walt to help on the farm. As always, Elias reacted to stress with his temper. He criticized and punished the children for misdeeds they didn't realize they'd committed. Walt argued with his father and complained, "What did I do? I can't read your mind."

A few weeks after his oldest sons moved out, Elias and his neighbor Coffman formed a local chapter of the American Society of Equity, a farmers' union. Elias began calling himself a Socialist and preached non-stop to anyone about what he believed was a fairer system of government. He went so far as bringing hobos home for supper in order to talk socialism with them. However, Flora wisely fed these visitors outside on the steps.

Walt was enrolled in Park School in September 1909. His mother had held him back until he was 7 years old so he could accompany his little sister, Ruth. He was embarrassed to be the oldest kid in class but soon got over it because he didn't have much interest in school anyway. He was more interested in making his classmates laugh, even at the risk of getting a caning.

The start of school also meant that Elias's two remaining sons were rarely available to help him with farm work. As idyllic as life on the farm could be, it became an impossible financial situation. With Elias's lack of farming skills plus the recently falling crop prices, the farming business was clearly becoming an unsustainable struggle. Then Elias contracted typhoid and after that pneumonia. Flora blamed his ill health on stress and insisted that they sell the farm.

Consequently, on the cold winter morning of November 28, 1910, the family auctioned the farm along with its stock and equipment for $5,175. After fewer than five years, Walt's blissful rural life had ended. He hugged his 6-month-old colt and cried when it was led away, hitched to the rig of its new owner.

The family moved into Marceline and lived in a small four-room house at 508 Kansas Avenue while the children finished the school year, and Elias recovered his health.

After six months, on May 17, 1911, they moved 120 miles southwest to Kansas City, Missouri, where they rented a house at 2706 East Thirty-first Street. It was a small house in a working-class neighborhood and so close to the street that they had to keep the curtains closed to prevent pedestrians from looking in.

The only thing the children liked about their new house was that it was close to the Fairmount amusement park. They couldn't afford to go inside the park, but they loved staring through the fence at this out-of-reach fairyland.

In September, Walt started at Benton Grammar School. Although he had completed second grade in Marceline, the new school wouldn't accept this and required that he repeat the grade. This meant he was now two or three years older than his classmates.

Elias purchased a paper route with 650 subscribers, earning from it about $31 a week. It was a pro-Republican paper, and soon Elias forgot his socialism and became a Conservative.

Nine-year-old Walt also helped deliver the papers. He left before dawn to make morning deliveries and didn't return home from his evening deliveries until dark. And Walt wasn't paid for this; it was strictly to help the family. To earn his own money, he got extra papers and sold them to commuters and secretly took an after-school job in a candy store.

Elias continued to save as much as he could from his paper route, and by September 1914, the family was able to afford a small frame house four blocks away, at 3028 Bellefontaine Street. It was great to have a home of their own, but to Walt, it was a grim and solemn place which never felt much like home.

This is because, although it was one thing to be hardworking and serious-minded, Elias was also kind of "churchy" as people used to say, and he didn't approve of any form of entertainment. Walt escaped this austere environment as much as he could by spending time two doors up the street at the home of his friend, Walt Pfeiffer.

The Pfeiffer's house was a happy place. Walt told his friend that he considered this his "real" family. Fun was just natural for the Pfeiffers. The family relished their playtime together and usually spent evenings sharing fun activities, such as playing the piano and singing or acting out little comedy sketches. Although very busy with school and work, Walt never missed an opportunity to hang out with the Pfeiffers, even if it meant sneaking out of a window at night. Walt Disney and Walt Pfeiffer became inseparable.

The boys also performed at school. They formed a comedy act, calling themselves the "Two Bad Walters," and one time they won 25 cents for placing fifth in a talent contest. Walt discovered that he enjoyed acting. He also loved the applause and the prize money.

He liked performing, but his school work continued to suffer. His exhausting paper-delivery schedule may have been part of the reason, or perhaps it was a simple lack of interest. He preferred to be acting or drawing ... and he drew non-stop. Instead of listening to his teacher, he would draw at his desk behind his propped-up textbook. Sometimes he sketched in the margins of his books and created animations by flipping through the pages.

As Walt's artwork improved, people took notice. The local barber, Bert Hudson, offered the young artist 10 cents or free haircuts in exchange for drawings to hang in his barbershop window.

Walt continuously strove to develop his talent. When he picked up papers to deliver, he usually stopped to observe the newspaper's cartoonists as they worked. Elias didn't understand his son's passion, but when Walt was 14 his father allowed him to attend the Saturday drawing class at the Kansas City Art Institute.

In June 1917, Walt graduated from the Benton School after completing seventh grade. Along with his diploma, the principal, James Cottingham, handed him a $7 prize for a comic character he'd drawn for the school.

Soon after, the family began to go their separate ways. Roy joined the navy to fight in The Great War. Elias sold his paper route, and he and Flora returned to Chicago where Elias worked at a company he'd been buying stock in, the O-Zell Jelly & Fruit Juice Company. Walt stayed behind to train the new paper route owner and moved in with Uncle Herbert and his wife and 1-year-old daughter.

After he trained the buyer of the paper route, Walt took a job selling papers, candy, soda, and tobacco on the Santa Fe Railway train. He loved riding the train, was fascinated by the plush velvet world of the Pullman sleeper cars, and enjoyed the scenery in all the states the train traveled through.

This job also taught him about the business world, including how some people might take advantage of, or steal from him if he wasn't careful. After two months, he quit the job to rejoin his parents in their house on Ogden Street on Chicago's West Side.

In September 1918, Walt was a freshman at William McKinley High School a few blocks from home. But school still couldn't hold his attention. He continued to spend most of his class time drawing.

He joined the school paper, The Voice, as a cartoonist, and the paper's manager wrote notes for Walt to be excused from class to draw for the paper. Since this was during the war, many of the cartoons were political, commenting on the German Kaiser or on the patriotism of the American fighting men.

Walt sometimes played hooky from school to go to the Art Institute or watch the artists draw at the newspaper office. He was a fan of Carey Orr, a cartoonist at the Chicago Tribune, and he attended some of Orr's classes at the Chicago Academy of Fine Arts.

Walt worked after school part-time for his father at the jelly factory. Sarah Scrogin, the wife of O-Zell's president, encouraged his art by buying some of his artwork, and asking him to draw posters for the company picnic.

Walt continued to think that his calling might be acting, and teamed up with another freshman, Russell Maas. They form a comedy act, performed with phony Dutch accents, but never succeeded at auditions for the local theater.

But one thing mattered more to Walt than acting or art, and that was the war. It was on everyone's mind, every day. Walt was only 16, but he was ashamed for not being in the war like his brother Roy. This may have been patriotism, but it was at least partly the sharp uniforms and military bands that were out every day encouraging men to enlist.

The summer after his freshman year, Walt decided he wasn't going back to school. Instead, he and Maas would join the navy. However, they were turned away for being too young. Next, they tried the Canadian forces, but Maas was rejected for poor eyesight and although Walt could qualify, he didn't want to go to war without his friend.

In July, Walt left his job at O-Zell, and he and Maas started working as substitute mail carriers. After he delivered the mail, he worked at a second job as a gateman on the subway, loading cars and closing the doors. It was a thrill for him to ride the subway, but between his two jobs, his work-days were more than 12 hours long.

On September 3, 1918, Walt had a close brush with death as he was leaving the post office to go to his subway job. Just as he exited the Chicago Federal Building, a massive explosion erupted behind him.

Hoping to free their union leader from the prison on the eighth floor, radicals of the left-wing Industrial Workers of the World labor union had set off a bomb. Walt was unhurt, but 30 people were injured, and four killed, including a man who worked only two desks from Walt's.

But he was unphased by the bombing and continued visiting the Federal Building, trying to get more mail routes or other odd jobs that paid 40 cents an hour.

Still disappointed in their attempts to join the service, Maas came up with the idea that they might be able to join the Red Cross Ambulance Corps. Maas had heard the Red Cross accepted applicants at 17, rather than 18 required by the military.

However, they were only sixteen — still too young, and anyway, Elias refused to give his permission. He said it would be like signing his son's death certificate.

But Flora finally relented to her son's pleading, signing her name and forging her husband's signature. Then she helped Walt convert the last digit on his birth certificate to read 1900 instead of 1901.

Walt was inducted into the Ambulance Corps and assigned to a training facility on Chicago's South Side near the University of Chicago. Within days, he contracted influenza in a horrifying epidemic that eventually took 20 million lives worldwide. Hospitals were now considered to be unsafe, so he was sent home. By the time he recovered three weeks later, his ambulance company had already sailed for France.

He returned to camp on November 4 and waited to be transported with the Automotive Mechanical Section. But then he heard that an armistice had been signed: The war was over, and he'd missed it.

Just when he thought he'd be sent home again, Walt was assigned to a group of 50 men to go to France and aid in the occupation. The next morning, he was on his way, traveling on a converted cattle boat, the Vaubin, which was loaded with ammunition.

Walt celebrated his 17th birthday on the way to France and arrived in Cherbourg on November 30. He was transferred at least a half-dozen times in the next two weeks before finally ending up at Hospital No. 102 in Neufchateau, 150 miles east of Paris. His Red Cross tasks at this post mostly involved running errands for the canteen, such as collecting eggs from nearby farms or delivering food to picnics for dignitaries.

While in France, he continued to draw. For the canteen, he did posters and menu illustrations. He painted designs on the sides of ambulances, charged other enlistees for personal caricatures, and sent editorial cartoons to the McKinley Voice and friends back home.

In November 1919, after a year in France, Walt was returned to Chicago. He went to Kansas City where he tried unsuccessfully to get hired by the Kansas City Star. Then he heard of an opening at the Pesmen-Rubin Art Studio. He brought samples of work he'd done in Paris and even offered to work a trial week for free.

They hired him for $50 a month to do advertising layouts. Here he became friends with 18-year-old Ubbe "Ub" Iwerks, a shy son of German immigrants. Six weeks later when the Christmas rush ended, both of them were laid off and out of work again.

Walt went back to work at the post office but continued improving his portfolio in the evenings. In his six weeks at the ad company, he had learned many new techniques, and he used these to polish his samples.

In early 1920, Walt and Ub started an art company they called Iwerks-Disney Commercial Artists. After two months of struggling with their new business, Walt saw an ad by the Kansas City Film Ad Company for an artist job that paid $40 a week. Ub insisted that Walt should be the one to take the job. Without the more out-going Walt as the salesman, Iwerks-Disney went out of business within weeks, but Walt convinced the ad company to also hire his friend.

The ad company created simple animations with stop-motion photography of paper dolls on wooden dowels. They produced inexpensive, one-minute films that were used by local theaters. Walt had always been captivated by animation, and he studied their process to learn everything he could. Then he added his own improvements to make the animations appear to move more fluidly.

But there was a limit to what could be done with cut-outs. Walt tried to convince his boss to try a new process called celluloid animation. This was an invention by John Randolph Bray, who also lived in Kansas City. It was a process where the artist would draw directly on layers of clear material. Walt's boss agreed to lend him a camera so that he could experiment with celluloid animation, but only after work on his own time.

With this camera, Walt developed a series of animations he called Bobby Bumps. These shorts were played at the Newman Theater where they called them Laugh-O-Grams. The theater's owner, Milton Feld, hired him to make twelve more shorts.

Although Walt was paid for this work, he still lost money on the deal by underestimating his costs. But his popular animations soon led to additional jobs, and he used the money to buy a camera. He now had a camera, the necessary skills, and customers.

At 19 years old, Walt Disney was ready to open his own studio.

~~~ IMAGINATION ~~~

Walt Disney taught the world to use their imagination, and that life wasn't only about serious pursuits, but sometimes about imaginary characters and magical kingdoms. One of his greatest strengths was his ability to retain the fervor and joy of his childhood — a childhood of farm animals, trains, and a small mid-century town — and then to infuse his imaginative creations with the sweet extracts of these memories.

As a child he was always too distracted with drawing to pay attention in school, but although not accumulating much of the intended school knowledge, he was collecting a rich store of fanciful cartoon characters often based on people in his life.

His five boyhood years on the farm — the people, events, animals, and places — were all firmly planted in his fertile imagination. An imagination shared with children and adults around the world. A rich imagination that was truly Walt Disney's happiest place in the world.

Albert Einstein

March 14, 1879 – April 18, 1955

"Authority is the greatest enemy of truth."
— Albert Einstein

In 1905, while working in the Swiss patent office, 26-year-old Albert Einstein had his miracle year, producing four ground-breaking articles that changed science and the world.

- He applied the quantum theory to light to explain the photoelectric effect, in which a material emits electrically charged particles when hit by light.
- He demonstrated experimental proof of the existence of atoms by analyzing the phenomenon of Brownian motion, in which tiny particles are seen to move when suspended in water.
- He introduced his special theory of relativity, which holds that the laws of physics are the same even for objects moving in different inertial frames (at constant speeds relative to each

other) and that the speed of light is a constant in all inertial frames.

He showed the fundamental relationship between mass and energy, concepts viewed previously as separate from each other. Einstein expressed this relationship with his famous equation: $E = mc^2$.

But what does this mean to you? Well, the following are just a few of the everyday things we enjoy that wouldn't be possible without Albert Einstein's discoveries.

- Aerosol cans
- Automatic supermarket doors
- Burglar alarms
- Carbon dating
- Cell phones
- Computers
- Digital cameras
- Digital clocks
- GPS
- Lasers
- Nuclear energy
- PET scans
- Semiconductors
- Smoke detectors
- Solar panels
- Television
- Weather forecasting

Besides making his own discoveries, Albert Einstein also restored scientists' belief in the power of reason and intellect, by changing the way they think about science. Before Einstein, scientists believed their job was limited to examining and explaining those phenomena which they could directly observe. Einstein demonstrated how they could use thought experiments to explore even the unobservable.

One of Einstein's thought experiments showed why there's a maximum speed limit in the universe, that light always moves at precisely this speed, that light travels in little bundles of energy he called "quanta," and that gravity is a curvature of spacetime.

He also demonstrated the fragility of scientific knowledge and showed scientists how to overcome their confirmation bias and critically reevaluate previously accepted concepts.

So, who was this person who catapulted mankind into the future we enjoy today — this man whose very name is synonymous with genius?

The truly meaningful answers are mostly obscured by the myths and legends surrounding his life. As Einstein said, "Everyone likes me, yet nobody understands me." But perhaps the story of his childhood will give us some revealing clues.

It's a story of how the unquenchable curiosity of a young boy led to the solutions of some of the universe's most profound mysteries.

The first mystery for Einstein, and the one that occupied his mind the most, was that of light. He puzzled over exactly what it was, and then how it always appeared to be moving at the same speed?

~~~

Friday, March 14, 1879

It was a beautiful almost-spring day, with a temperature of 45º Fahrenheit, a cloudless blue sky, and a light breeze. At 11:30 a.m., in a well-heated apartment at the edge of the Swabian city of Ulm, Albert Einstein was born.

His parents, Hermann and Pauline, wanted to name their baby Abraham, after Hermann's father. But they worried the name would mark the child as too obviously Jewish, so they decided at least Albert could share his grandfather's initials.

Albert was the couple's first child, but when he was born, they felt something wasn't right. The back of their baby's head was much larger and more angular than normal. This may not have been a problem but any deformity was cause for concern because at that time, infant mortality was still a major problem.

Other than his misshaped head though, the boy seemed healthy and active, and according to Hermann's mother when she first saw him, "Much too fat! Much too fat!"

The family resided in a four-story residential building on the corner at Bahnhofstrasse B 135. Their home was only a few feet from the Ulm train station where the new Lightning Express stopped on its way between Paris and Istanbul.

Ulm was an industrial town of 33,000 inhabitants, in the Baden-Wurttemberg region of southwest Germany, on the Danube River. Generations of Einsteins had lived in this area, but Germany as a nation didn't exist until eight years before Albert's birth. For centuries, the German-speaking region had no central government and was simply a loose alliance of kingdoms and cities.

In 1871, Otto Von Bismarck formed the German Empire and appointed himself Imperial Chancellor after convincing the German states to rally under the patriotic banner of German identity, and to fight a war with France deliberately provoked for this purpose.

Ironically, the town of Ulm already had a historical connection with mathematics. In fact, their motto was "Ulmenses sunt mathematici," "Mathematicians, one and all," a remark attributed to their famous native son, the mathematical wizard Johannes Faulhaber, creator of the Faulhaber's Formula, a method for calculating the sums of powers of positive integers.

Albert's father, Hermann, showed a considerable talent for math when he was young. But in his youth, Jews in the area were only allowed to practice skilled trades, and opportunities for advanced studies were limited.

Hermann Einstein and Pauline Koch were married in 1876, in the Cannstatt synagogue near Stuttgart, when he was 29, and she was 18. Albert was born in their third year of marriage.

Hermann worked as a salesman for a feather bed company he co-owned with his cousin. Hermann was intelligent and industrious, but also quiet and somewhat passive, so not well suited for sales.

Pauline was a vibrant and outgoing young woman whose father was a prosperous corn-merchant in Stuttgart. People considered her to be more practical and forthright than her husband, but different as they were in many ways, theirs was a happy marriage.

Life in Ulm wasn't much different from that of previous generations. The background sounds of the city were still hoofbeats and steam engines. The houses were lighted with gas or oil and heated with wood or coal. Transportation was by horse, train, or the newly popular bicycle, and communication was via telegraph or mail.

But in 1879, this timeless world was sitting at the edge of dramatic change. The pace of technological and scientific advancements was accelerating; recent advances in the fight against pathogens and improvements in hygiene were leading to rapid population growth in Europe; and in December of that year, Thomas Edison publicly demonstrated his first successful light bulb.

Life wasn't easy for the Einstein family though. Soon after Albert was born, his father's feather bed business suffered major setbacks. Hermann was getting nervous about his ability to support his wife and son.

Fortunately, Hermann's younger brother Jakob came to the rescue with the suggestion that the two of them start an electrical equipment company. With Edison's new electric lights and generators, cities were clamoring for the electrification of industries, for new mass transit vehicles, and for street lighting.

In June 1880, the Einsteins moved to Munich where Hermann and Jakob formed a company called Elektrotechnische Fabrik J. Einstein & Cie. They manufactured and sold electrical equipment that used Edison's direct current. Jakob, the only one in the family to attend university, had a degree in engineering and he handled the technical aspects of the business. Hermann secured their government and business contracts.

Their electrical business was an enormous success, adding much of the new lighting to the streets of Munich. This new prosperity soon allowed the Einstein family to purchase a large house in one of Munich's middle-class suburbs.

In this house, on November 18, 1881, Albert's younger sister, Marie was born. Two-year-old Albert adored his baby sister, and "Maja," as he called her, became Albert's lifelong friend.

Although Albert's head remained larger than average, at least the shape had become normal. But now his parents had a new worry because he wasn't developing like other babies. He seemed physically healthy, but he wasn't speaking or babbling like other children his age. With his larger than average head and lack of speech, the family housekeeper suggested that the boy was probably retarded. His parents took their son to a doctor, seeking a diagnosis, but the doctor had no explanation.

Finally, when Albert was 3, he began speaking. However, his speech was unusually slow because he first stared blankly while forming the sentences in his head, and then moved his lips while silently mouthing them, before finally uttering them aloud.

Another big concern for his parents were his frequent and sudden bursts of anger. Until he was about 7 years old, he was easily provoked into violent temper tantrums. His face changed color, and he threw things at his tutor or Maja, sometimes causing injuries, and some tutors left and refused to return.

Even when not frightening others away, young Albert was a loner who had little interest in playing with other children. He preferred a self-imposed isolation, wrapped up in private puzzle games, or engaged in daydreaming or meditative musings.

When Albert was 5 years old, he encountered something he found so incredible, his whole body shook. He was lying sick in bed and his father brought a compass to entertain him and distract him from his illness. The moment Albert took this compass in his hand became a turning point in his life. He was shocked and mystified that the needle could move with nothing touching it and he shuddered as he pondered the invisible force acting on the needle.

The needle's behavior conflicted with the young boy's understanding of nature, and he realized something hidden had to be causing the action.

The realization suddenly dawned on him that there must be more to the universe than what he could experience with his senses.

As a toddler, it was already clear that Albert was an intelligent and inquisitive boy. So, although there was a Jewish school nearby, On October 1, 1885, his parents enrolled him in the Petersschule Catholic school because they thought it had a better academic program.

Hermann and Pauline were Ashkenazi Jews by heritage, but they didn't practice their religion. In fact, Hermann referred to religious ceremonies as ancient superstitions. Regardless of Albert's heritage, at his new school, he became interested in, and excelled at his compulsory Catholic studies.

However, Albert was still technically Jewish. Even though religion was rarely discussed in his home and Albert had given it little thought, it now complicated his life in school. His teachers were kind to their only Jewish student, but many of the children came from homes with strong anti-Semitic prejudices and these children repeatedly bullied Albert on his way home.

To keep Albert busy at home, his mother decided he should study music. She arranged for violin lessons and at first, Albert rebelled. He didn't want to learn music and he especially disliked the necessary memorization.

But his mother persisted and eventually Albert got to the point where he enjoyed his violin and found that the study of music also fit with his natural tenacity and strong self-discipline. As he got better at the violin, he developed an admiration for Mozart's sonatas and pretty soon he couldn't imagine life without playing music.

Like his music and puzzle games, Albert's outside pastimes were also typically solitary, such as constructing elaborate structures with his blocks in his backyard.

He also enjoyed spending time with his family, especially long hikes in the foothills of the Alps. He loved walking and being close to nature where he could let his mind wander.

Albert's best friends were his thoughts; He was happiest when he was either discovering something: such as the solution to a puzzle game or the mysteries of a compass, or when he was creating something: such as music or towers of blocks.

Another astonishing discovery was when his Uncle Caesar Koch visited from Brussels and brought Albert a toy steam engine. The fire from the little pellets, heated the water in the boiler, and the resulting steam that pushed the piston which spun the wheel. This encounter was Albert's first glimpse into the connection between heat and force, and as with the compass, it set his mind to work trying to understand it.

By the time Albert was 6 years old, his mother recognized what a uniquely cerebral and curious child he was and would tell him that someday he'd be a great professor. She was proud of her bright little boy and provided as much support as she could by showing appreciation and encouragement for all his interests and accomplishments. Hermann, on the other hand, was content to simply observe his son without hoping for anything more.

Growing up around his father's electrical business gave Albert a firsthand look at the potential of science and technology. He also learned from frequent conversations he had with his Uncle Jakob, who had a special knack for explaining complex abstract topics in a playful manner, and used clever metaphors to make mathematics easier to conceptualize. He introduced Albert to algebra, describing it as a hunt: "When the animal we're hunting cannot be caught, we temporarily call it X, and continue to hunt until it is bagged."

Albert struggled though, with rote memorization, and considered his memory one of his greatest weaknesses. But when teaching the boy mathematics, Uncle Jakob made it easier to remember by giving the boy a firm understanding of the concepts involved. As a result, when Jakob showed him the Pythagorean theorem, the 8-year-old boy plunged into the task of solving it, and in three weeks deduced a correct proof of the theorem on his own.

Jakob also supplied Albert with the textbooks that would be used in his upcoming math and science classes. Albert typically read the books and completed the work before the term began, which meant he could ignore the lessons during class and focus on his own thoughts, while still getting top grades on tests. This approached fitted well with his preference for independence; doing things his way instead of following instructions. Of course, his inattentiveness in class exasperated his teachers.

Even though class was a bore for Albert, he found the study of math to be a joy. He found the clear and logical structure of math was as fascinating as it was in music. His parents continued to supply him with advanced math books, and he continued teaching himself during evenings and summers.

During these studies, Albert would become completely absorbed, in a world of his own, and oblivious to the chaos and noise around him. At every opportunity, he wanted to sit quietly and work on his mathematical challenges. His sister teased him that he looked like an absent-minded Buddha as he sat on the couch in his trancelike state, meditating on one of his problems.

In 1888, Albert completed elementary school. His overall grades were mediocre. But although an average student in most subjects, he was always first in mathematics class.

In October, he transferred to the Luitpold Gymnasium, which was the equivalent of today's high school. The school assigned a teacher to give their few Jewish students instruction in Judaism. Albert embraced these studies with enthusiasm, and although it posed a bit of an inconvenience for the rest of his non-practicing family, he became observant of Jewish religious practices, including eating Kosher, and observing the Sabbath.

After the ostracism he experienced in his previous school, he flung himself into Judaism to feel a sense of pride in himself and his heritage. Another motivation for his interest in religion may have been to find explanations for the invisible forces of nature that continued to perplex him.

At the new school, discipline was more strictly enforced than at his elementary school. Albert's instinctive opposition to discipline now grew stronger. He compared his teachers to drill sergeants, and complained to them about their "mindless and mechanical teaching methods," which he said, "caused him great difficulty" because of his "poor memory for words." As he declared to one teacher who threatened him with punishment, "I would rather let all kinds of punishment descend upon me than learn to rattle something off by heart."

In truth, Luitpold was one of the more progressive schools of the time and had no intention of breaking the spirit of its students. But Albert adamantly preferred independent thought and discovery over following the instructions of others.

This attitude wasn't restricted to school. In daily life, Albert also rebelled against authority, whether it came from rigid rules, the dictates of bourgeois life, dress codes, dogmatisms of religion or science, militarism, nationalism, or government ideology.

Albert's opposition to authority was one of his most significant personality traits. It was his permanent rebellious, and his carefree, child-like manner that allowed him to freely ponder the nature and mysteries of the universe without being constrained by the tyranny of existing knowledge.

In 1889, the Einstein family adopted the Jewish tradition of inviting "needy young religious scholars" for a meal on the Sabbath. But because the family wasn't strictly observant, they invited a Jewish student from Poland who was attending a nearby medical school to eat with them on Thursdays. This student was Max Talmud.

When they met, Max was 21 and Albert was 10. During his visits, Max talked to Albert about the physics he was studying in medical school. When Max saw how keenly interested the young boy was, he lent him his 21-volume series of *The People's Books on Natural Science*, by Aaron Bernstein.

One of Bernstein's ideas was particularly striking to Albert's imagination. Bernstein asked readers to imagine being on a speeding train and then imagine a bullet was shot straight into one of the windows. The bullet would appear as if it were shot at an angle, because the train would move between the time the bullet entered one window and exited the opposite one. Bernstein said the same should be true of light going through a telescope as the earth moved through space. Therefore, both the bullet and the light would necessarily travel faster through space to cover the longer angled distance. However, light always seemed to move at the same speed, whether you're standing motionless or sitting in a speeding train.

Albert was captivated by Bernstein's thoughts about the speed of light always appearing the same regardless of the speed of the observer passing through it, and greatly enjoyed discussing this strange concept with Max. Albert truly savored this opportunity to have someone he could talk with about the many fascinating topics that always intrigued him.

From these studies though, and their deep intellectual incursions into the nature of the universe, Albert began to question his religion. This was an uncomfortable experience for the 12-year-old boy. It was disconcerting but cathartic, and finally convinced him that many stories in the Bible couldn't possibly be true. This unavoidable conclusion made a crushing impression on the boy and ended his practice of Judaism.

But this experience also opened new windows in his mind. As he entered his teens, Albert began questioning everything. He binged on freethinking; exploring more areas of interest, and becoming more enthusiastically involved in his private studies.

He also continued his music studies and the more he learned, the more profound his love became for the music of Mozart and Beethoven, which he relentlessly tried to duplicate on his violin. What began as a chore, his violin practice was now a delight, and was also an ideal way to relax and unwind, even while firmly concentrating on his technique.

In his advanced math studies, with Max's help, Albert learned Euclidean geometry, and then calculus. But by the time Albert was 13,

Max had run out of math and science to teach the boy. So, Max began tutoring Albert in philosophy, giving him *Critique of Pure Reason*, by Immanuel Kant. Albert read the book, and this led to further interesting conversations to share with Max.

Albert's friendship with Max, and their scientific and philosophical discussions, weren't only an enjoyable pastime. These exchanges also laid much of the foundation for many ideas and concepts that captivated Albert's mind for years to come.

By the age of 15, he was continuing his math studies on his own, teaching himself differential and integral calculus. These were obviously complex concepts for a young boy to master. As a method to clear his mind and free his imagination, he liked to construct houses of cards — sometimes up to 14 stories high — or take long walks in the nearby woods.

As curious and hungry to learn as this boy was, school continued to be a tedious and tiresome experience. Even with his excellent grades in math and science, Albert had difficulty staying focused in the classroom. He felt stifled by the rigid curriculum that seemed to squeeze all the joy and creative expression out of education.

And these were also opinions he freely shared with his teachers. Because he never hesitated to criticize his teachers, their rules, and their curriculum, his fellow students called Albert "Biedermeier" or "Honest John." Beider referred to someone who's honest and trustworthy to the point of being naive, and Meier is a ubiquitous name, like calling someone a plain-Jane.

Albert's teachers outside of his math and science classes, concluded that he was just slow, this opinion being further reinforced by his stubborn silence whenever they disciplined him.

But this 15-year-old boy couldn't see the purpose of his classes. What were his teachers trying to accomplish? If they were trying to educate him, what was education? If it was learning to think, then, what was thinking?

To Albert, "thinking" must be more than simply experiencing new sense impressions. Even categorizing new information was simply a form of memorization.

He decided that real thinking only occurs when an idea connects to multiple categories so that these separate categories develop new connections through this idea. These new connections then expose the mind to new and previously unconsidered perspectives and concepts. This type of epiphany usually arises when new experiences come into conflict with previously accepted ideas.

This process usually occurs subconsciously without words, causing these mental breakthroughs to seem to appear spontaneously.

None of this was happening in school. To Albert, education was experiencing the wonder of discovery through the application of your intelligence, and he decided that real education was only be possible once you forgot what you'd memorized in school.

To Albert, the first ingredient of education was imagination, not facts. As he sometimes recommended to people who later inquired about his intelligence, "To be intelligent, read fairy tales. If you want to be more intelligent, then read *more* fairy tales."

Albert's disillusionment with school wasn't only about education. Something more profound and disturbing was upsetting him: He was depressed by the Bismarckian militarism that had recently pervaded German society. The unquestioning reverence for authority and chain of command that had become so popular in schools seemed to mimic military discipline. The sight of his fellow students playing soldiers and marching to drum beats during breaks was ugly and offensive to him. Although he had always been a pacifist, his recent disenchantment with religion increased his suspicion of arbitrary authority, blind obedience, and mechanical discipline.

At the same time that Albert was dealing with frustrations at school, life at home was becoming stressful as his father's electrical business began failing. His father and uncle were losing business to companies that were working with Tesla's new alternating current. Hermann and Jakob's direct current equipment was becoming outdated, and they couldn't afford to convert their operations to the new technology.

Jakob left the company to work as an engineer for a larger firm, but Hermann decided to start yet another electrical supply company, this time in Italy. Therefore, Albert's father, mother, and sister moved to Milan, where Hermann hoped he could still market his direct current products, and Albert was left behind to live with distant relatives while he finished school.

He continued working towards a degree in electrical engineering to honor his father's wishes. But school was becoming unbearable. His teachers sensed that Albert felt a superiority of mind and detected what seemed like quiet contempt. He sat in the back of his classes, lost in his thoughts until a teacher tried to catch him by suddenly calling on him to answer a question in front of the class. Without hesitation, Albert would scribble the correct equations on the blackboard amidst the surprise and snickers of the other students, which further exasperated his teachers.

One of his teachers, Dr. Joseph Degenhart, went so far as to suggest that perhaps Albert should leave the school. Albert answered, "But I haven't done anything wrong." To which the teacher replied, "Your mere presence spoils the respect of the class for me."

Whether or not this suggestion was serious, Albert decided to follow it and devised a plan to leave school for good. He obtained a letter from his mathematics teacher, Joseph Ducrue, explaining that Albert had already reached the level of a graduating senior. As an excuse to leave school, Albert obtained a written diagnosis from Max Talmud's older brother, who was the Einsteins' family's doctor, stating that he was suffering from nervous exhaustion.

Albert then boarded a train to Italy, showed up unannounced at his parents' door, and declared that he would never return to Germany. Furthermore, he requested that his father help him renounce his German citizenship to avoid the military conscription he faced in two years.

His parents were disappointed that their son was a high school dropout. But Albert explained that with his letters of recommendation, he had already persuaded the Swiss Federal Polytechnic School in Zurich, Switzerland, to accept him, despite the fact he was just 16 years old. He only needed to pass their admissions test.

For the next 10 months, Albert lived with his parents while he studied for the exam, during which time he also assisted his father with technical work at his electric company.

However, he failed the exam, mainly due to trouble he had with French and botany. But the examining professor, Heinrich Friedrich Weber, was so impressed with Albert's understanding of physics that he made an exception. He told Albert that he could still enroll in the school if he first attended the Swiss Cantonal in the nearby town of Aarau to complete his secondary studies.

In October 1895, Albert started this new school. While living in Aarau, he boarded in the home of Jost Winteler, his wife Pauline, and their daughter Marie, who was two years older than Albert. Mr. Winteler was a professor at the school, and he agreed to tutor Albert in the subjects Albert found most difficult, such as French, chemistry, and biology.

Albert did better in this new school. It had a less coercive climate than his old high school and was more tolerant of new ideas. Its teaching methods were based on the philosophy of the Swiss educational reformer Johann Henrich Pestalozzi, who encouraged the use of intuition, conceptual thinking, and visual imagery. This was much closer to what Albert thought a school should be.

During his studies, he came across a book that proposed an interesting thought experiment about electricity. It suggested imagining yourself riding alongside electricity as it traveled through a wire.

But Albert had been curious about light since he was a child, and so instead wondered what it would be like to ride alongside a beam of light. This speculation turned into an unyielding fascination that continued to command his attention for years: What would the light look like? How would it react? If light were a wave, would the wave appear to be standing still? It was a difficult thing to imagine, but it was a mystery impossible for him to ignore.

Constantly consumed with such scientific curiosity, Albert read every science journal he could get his hands on. Then, while still only 16, he decided to chronicle some of his own ideas, producing his first scientific paper, titled "The Investigation of the State of Aether in Magnetic Fields."

But his interests at the Wintelers weren't confined only to science. While boarding with the family, Marie and Albert developed a mutual attraction, which over the year grew into something deeper. Both sets of parents approved of the relationship, and in fact, were certain the two would marry.

But at the end of the year, after finishing school with the highest possible grades in every subject except French, he forced himself to say goodbye to Marie and left for Zurich to enroll in the Polytechnic.

Hermann wanted Albert to be an engineer like his uncle, but Albert couldn't imagine that career. He was always more attracted to theory than to practicalities. He wanted to think for the sake of thinking, just as he played music for the sake of music, and not with a goal of earning money. He decided to pursue a teaching diploma in mathematics and physics.

At the university, he was able to focus on the types of things that interested him most, making his years there among the happiest of his life. At the Polytechnic, he made deep and lasting friendships with like-minded people with whom he could indulge in long conversations on topics that intrigued him most, such as light, time and space.

He enjoyed spending afternoons at the coffee shop, engaging in discussions with other students. However, he continued to have difficulties obeying authority, and would skip lectures he was less interested in, and threw instructions in the trash to perform classroom experiments his own way.

When he left Marie, he had promised to write regularly, and during his first months at school, he did. But over time, his letters became shorter and less frequent, until they ended altogether when he met someone new.

That someone was Mileva Marić, the only woman enrolled in the Polytechnic. Albert and Mileva began as study partners, and it was soon apparent that Mileva was quite brilliant. Before long, he believed himself to be romantically attracted to her and decided she was the woman he would marry.

But Mileva wanted to keep their relationship platonic. She didn't want anything to disrupt the education her father had worked so hard to provide for her. Therefore, she decided to distance herself, by transferring to Heidelberg University in Germany.

While they were apart, Albert and Mileva exchanged many long letters. The letters though, contained little romantic content, consisting primarily of discussions about school lectures or the workings of the universe. However, their friendship continued to deepen, and Albert began asking Mileva to return to Zurich. In April 1896, she agreed, and soon after returning, the two became inseparable.

The match was a surprise to Albert's friends. By his later teens, Albert had changed quite a bit. He was still a loner, but he had overcome his childhood shyness. He had also grown into a strikingly handsome young man, one his friends thought could attract any woman he chose.

Mileva was three years older than Albert, and though not unattractive, she was rather plain looking, and so many of Albert's friends wondered why he was interested in her.

But Albert was deeply attracted to Mileva's intellect. She was one of the rare people in his life who was his intellectual equal. She understood those relentless fascinations that preoccupied his mind. With Mileva, he had someone he could discuss those ideas he'd been pondering all his life.

Questions like: "Mileva, how do you think it could be possible for light to always appear to be moving at the same speed, even to an observer who's moving through it?"

~~~ GENIUS ~~~

Albert Einstein's breakthrough theories on the nature of the universe made him the most famous "genius" of all time. Somehow, he had the ability to see what no one else could, to unravel mysteries that most others hadn't even considered. His antipathy for authority allowed him to see through the haze of the "settled science," and his childlike curiosity compelled him to continue searching for answers to these incomprehensible mysteries.

But how was he so smart? Did he develop his analytical powers through diligent effort? It's hard to fathom a level of genius like Albert Einstein's, so it's easy to conclude he must have been born with a special brain. Perhaps he was, we don't know. But not every seed sprouts.

A child born with a misshaped head, slow to speak, and prone to violent temper tantrums, could have been written off before his abilities were recognized. He could have been labeled — and then lived up (or "down"?) to this label. What would we label a child who can't pay attention in school, argues with the teacher, refuses to follow instructions, does poorly in most of his classes, and can't remember his lessons?

Fortunately though, for Albert Einstein — and the world — his loving, patient parents consistently endeavored to support and encourage their son's exceptional independence and curiosity.

Henry Ford

July 30, 1863 – April 7, 1947

The only real mistake is the one from which we learn nothing.
— Henry Ford

Henry Ford founded the Ford Motor Company on June 17, 1903. It was a factory to build cars. But was an entirely different type of factory, a factory built to maximize efficiency. Using conveyer-belt-driven assembly lines, Ford's company could to assemble an entire car in 93 minutes, making his cars less expensive and his workers more valuable.

This new mass production method was so successful that it was soon copied by other industries. In all sectors: manufacturing costs fell, causing existing products to become more affordable, and entirely new products to become feasible. The world was changing; arriving in a new century on the shores of the machine age.

Before Ford, most manufacturers relied on individual craftsmen to build complete assemblies on their own. With a division of labor, workers could now specialize in one portion of the process, becoming more expert and more valuable, and thus better paid.

These two effects: lower costs and higher pay, launched an unprecedented surge in the middleclass standard of living. A cornucopia of previously unaffordable or even non-existent products were now available to the average consumer.

The unprecedented deluge of motor vehicles also revolutionized the world of transportation and industry. Americans became more mobile, and so did the products they built. People could go where their talents were most valued, and the products they produced could go where they were most wanted.

It's difficult to overestimate the impact this one man's insistence on labor-saving efficiencies had on the U.S. standard of living — and soon on much of the world. Whether you're buying a Ford, a Chevrolet, a Chrysler ... or a dishwasher, you can be grateful for the genius and persistence of this man for the abundance of products now within your reach.

What inspired this man to mechanize the manufacturing process, replacing the age-old system of individual craftsmen with one of automation and specialization? In this story, you'll see how F80 acresocalled "laziness" drove this young boy to fall in love with the idea of efficient machinery, and in particular, the machines of transportation.

~~~

Thursday, July 30, 1863

America was still reverberating from the shocking news spilling out of Gettysburg, where three weeks earlier, the Union Army had thwarted Robert E. Lee's invasion of the North in a battle of unimaginable violence and bloodshed.

But on this peaceful summer's morning far from the war, on a quiet farm in Michigan, another world-changing event was taking place. At 7:00 a.m. before the morning sun had yet risen above the treetops, Henry Ford was born to William and Mary Ford. He was their first child.

Henry's father, William, was a man of medium height, wiry, with high cheekbones. He arrived in America with his parents in 1848, when he was 21. His family had immigrated from Ireland to escape the potato famine, and eventually settled in Michigan on a 160-acre farm.

William became a carpenter for the Michigan Central Railroad and began saving his earnings to buy his own farm. As was common among the Irish, he had a deep respect for the independence of landownership and farming.

William was also proud to live in America. As he explained it: "The great miracle of America is, it's a place where a man can own the land upon which he lives and works. In America, there's personal independence."

By September 15, 1858, he'd saved enough from his carpentry job to buy the southern 80 acres of his father's farm, for $600.

William also did occasional carpentry work for his neighbors, the O'Herns, and this is where he met and fell in love with the attractive, dark-eyed, Mary Litogot. Mary was the youngest child of Belgium immigrants and was orphaned by the accidental death of her father. She was then adopted and raised in the loving and affectionate home of Margaret and Patrick O'Hern.

William and Mary were married on April 25, 1861 and the newlyweds moved into the O'Herns' spacious 7-room house that William had helped build a few years earlier. The two families shared this home harmoniously and in 1867, William purchased the O'Hern's entire 91-acre estate, adding it to his own successful and prosperous farm.

The months leading up to Henry's birth were an anxious time for the couple because Mary had delivered a stillborn son in January of the previous year. Fortunately, these worries vanished when they saw their vigorous and healthy boy.

The William's farm was near Dearborn, a small town, 10 miles west of Detroit. At the time, the city of Detroit had a population of just 116,000. In fact, there were only 750,000 residents in the whole state. Michigan was still a new state, gaining statehood in 1837, 26 years before Henry's birth. Towns, villages, and rural communities were scattered throughout the state in a landscape thick with forests of oak, elm, maple, ash, beech, basswood, and pine. The new state was situated between the Great Lakes in the north, the Ohio River to the south, the Appalachians to the east, and the Great Plains to the west. Although farms were beginning to appear, much of the land was still frontier.

This quiet wilderness still couldn't escape the turbulence of the Civil War, and as a northern state, Michigan was swept up in the antislavery politics of the new Republican Party, with its motto of "free soil, free labor, free men."

But while the history of the country was being written in blood, daily life on the farm continued to revolve around the seasons and never-ending chores.

Over the next ten years, the family continued to grow, adding five more children. Each of them arrived two years apart: John in 1865, Margaret in 1867, Jane in 1869, William Jr. in 1871, and Robert in 1873.

It was a close-knit family, centered on farming and their home, with everyone working together under Mary's steadfast and methodical guidance. Family life in this farmhouse would always hold Henry's most treasured memories.

Henry Ford's Birthplace

Their home was warm and inviting, with crimson carpets, kerosene lamps, family china in the kitchen, and a Starlight Model 25 stove with its stacks of firewood out back. In the parlor was a foot-pump organ, around which the family gathered in the evening to sing hymns and favorite songs of the time, such as "Turkey in the Straw" and "Flow Gently Sweet Afton."

One of Henry's earliest memories took place in June 1866, when he was almost 3 years old. His father took him and his 1-year-old brother John to see a bird's nest he'd found under a large oak log about 20 yards from the house. William carried John, while Henry ran alongside. When they got there, what they saw was a nest with four eggs and a chirping song sparrow.

From this early encounter, Henry developed a life-long interest in birds. But he never developed a similar affinity for other animals. Despite growing up on a farm, he had no love of horses like most farm boys. And he hated cows. As for chickens — he wouldn't even eat them. He said they were only fit for hawks.

Still, Henry enjoyed rural life and its inherent virtues of self-sufficiency and independence. But Henry didn't like farm work. In fact, he was known to avoid labor whenever possible. As a neighbor who worked on the Ford farm described him: "That little devil was the laziest bugger on the face of the earth! Henry would work along all right until about ten o'clock in the morning, and then he would want to go to the house for a drink of water. He would go and get the drink of water, but he would never come back."

Henry tried to avoid work whenever he could, but his mother Mary was always reminding her children that life cannot be all fun. "You must earn the right to play," she would tell them. She insisted that work and play should be in proper proportion, and recreation was the reward for labor.

Even though Mary was a firm believer in the value of work, she was absolutely against wasted effort and took every opportunity to impress her children with the importance of working efficiently. Having a strong work ethic was important, but what you accomplished was more important than the amount of work you did. Henry was always impressed with his mother's passion for efficiency and admired the systematic and orderly way in which she did her chores.

Mary taught her children about more than work. She also showed them plenty of love and was openly affectionate. However, she never spoiled them, and was sure to let them know when they were wrong. She took a long-range view, doing what she considered best for her children's welfare, even if it meant they temporarily thought they "hated" her. Although the children complained when their mother was stern, they appreciated her steady hand guiding and protecting them, and this appreciation grew into a profound respect.

At the end of each day's work, the family typically read, played card games, or sang around the organ. Henry and his brothers sometimes wrestled or played harmless pranks on each other. Overall, the farm life of the children was one of sleigh bells, wood hauling, cold winters, setting suns, long walks, chilly weather, and playing with friends. On Sundays, the family attended the Christ Episcopal Church in Dearborn. They also liked to participate in neighborhood picnics and church socials.

One day, a German farm-hand, Adolf Culling was showing Henry his new watch, and took the back off to reveal how it worked. The boy was spell-bound. There, in that tiny machine, he witnessed a mechanical miracle: a rocking arm and the tiny cogs of the escapement wheel, working to steadily advance the hands of the watch, second by second, in perfect time. From this chance encounter, sprang Henry's preoccupation with all things mechanical. From this point on, his central interest became machines of all types.

Right away, Henry began seeking watches he could take apart and study. He even built his own set of tools by filing and hammering knitting needles into tiny screwdrivers and creating a pair of tweezers from one of his mother's corset stays. Now, the only toys he played with were tools. And no clock in the house was safe. As a neighbor put it, "Every clock in the Ford home shuddered when it saw Henry coming."

Henry's obsession with mechanical things also included the wind-up toys that belonged to his brothers and sisters. A joke in the household was when the children would surround their Christmas toys to protect them and say, "Don't let Henry have them. He just takes them apart."

Even if he was teased, Henry was proud of his mechanical abilities, and he always loved it when his mother called him a born mechanic.

To Henry, mechanical things weren't just remarkable in themselves: He saw automation as a way to ameliorate unnecessary human labor. Although he deserved his reputation for being lazy, it's also possible that what looked like laziness was his rebellion against wasted energy — something he, like his mother, detested. He regularly complained that there was too much work on the farm and that there must be better ways.

When Henry did his farm work, he always looked for methods or shortcuts he could use to lighten his chores. One of these was when he decided the farm gates were too troublesome to open and close. To solve this, he constructed new hinges for the gates and a device that allowed him to open and close the gates without getting down from his wagon.

Henry admired his mother's obsession with finding the easiest ways to accomplish work, and he clearly adopted this attitude as his own. One of the most cherished compliments he ever received was when an uncle told him, "You're just like your mother about efficiency." Nothing pleased him more than to be compared to his mother. He admired her work ethic and the intelligent approach she took to her chores. If he was compared to his mother, he knew he was doing all right.

This pride of work was the foundation of the cultural values of nineteenth-century America. It was a Victorian culture, which combined the principles of Protestant moralism, individualism, work ethic, and personal restraint. It promoted frugality and work, where an individual's labor could be turned into products for home, or to be sold.

Henry was also taught to complete his work with a cheerful attitude and was never offered sympathy if he complained about his chores. "Life will give you many unpleasant tasks to do; your duty will be hard and disagreeable and painful to you at times, but you must do it," his mother reminded him.

Henry's parents could be stern, but Henry was never physically punished. Instead, Mary used the Victorian method of shaming. Once when he was caught lying, she simply showed her disgust. He felt humiliated and considered this worse than a whipping. He had to live for days with the feeling of having done this despicable thing to his mother.

Other lessons came from the books his mother read to the children. Each night, she read from the Bible, *Pilgrim's Progress*, and sometimes *Gems of Life*, a collection of poems and inspirational essays.

One of the most lasting lessons Henry learned from his mother was the importance of harmony in the home. Mary strove to maintain balance and unity in the family and said that if they couldn't be happy at home, they'd never be happy anywhere.

Henry's father was also loving, but he tended to be more reserved in its expression. Although William wasn't as openly affectionate as Mary, he still had a warm relationship with his children. He was a kind and fair parent who believed that children should obey. But he combined this with more than the usual amount of tolerance. For example, although generally frowned upon by Protestants, he still allowed the children to play cards around the table in the evening. William was a quiet, hands-off parent, who usually only stepped in if the children got too rowdy or argumentative.

William also set a good example for his children by being well-informed. He subscribed to several newspapers, and he participated in the civic affairs of the community. He was a member of the school board, a road commissioner, and by the 1870s, a justice of the peace.

Everyone in town knew and liked William, and neighbors routinely brought things to him that needed fixing. William had a reputation as a good farmer and as someone who helped others when they were in need. He was a kind, considerate, and well-respected man, and by the time Henry was born, William was already a local self-made success story, who by then had increased his farm to 120 acres. He was even the first farmer in the Dearborn area to have a buggy.

Like most of his neighbors, who were staunch supporters of republicanism and classical liberalism, William was a firm believer in personal independence and the strong tradition of the individual farmer making the most of his labor and talents. He was a stalwart member of a proud rural community, populated with self-reliant landowners and fiercely independent citizens.

As a toddler, Henry loved following his father around, watching him work and wanting to "help." And William enjoyed spending this time with his son. William was skilled with tools, building and repairing things, and took every opportunity to pass these skills along to his son.

William's farm work lasted every day from sunrise to dark, after which he went home to do household chores. Work on the farm included growing wheat, corn, and hay; raising livestock and smoking meat, tending a fruit orchard, hunting and fishing, preserving vegetables in cellars over the winter and cutting firewood for the home or to sell in the city.

When William drove his wagon to Detroit, he frequently took his sons with him, and after the errands were done, he sometimes spent the afternoon showing them the sites of the city.

During these outings, Henry especially loved staring at the displays in the watchmaker's window. On one occasion, his father took him to see the railroad yards. While visiting the roundhouse, an engineer, Tommy Garrett, took the boy into his locomotive and showed him the levers and gauges, and explained how the firebox created steam and how the steam moved the pistons, which turned the wheels. This was the beginning of Henry's a fascination with steam engines.

But unlike his father, Henry didn't care much for land ownership and farming. He preferred machines and would rather skip farm chores to do something like watch a threshing machine. Henry's brother William Jr. described Henry as: "Oh, Henry ain't much of a farmer. He's more of a tinkerer."

Although William wanted Henry to concentrate on farm chores, he respected his son's interest in mechanics and gave him the use of a 12-by-16-foot shed to use as a workshop. One thing Henry used his workshop for was to repair his neighbors' watches. He didn't charge for this service but did it for his own satisfaction. And the neighbors were pleased because he usually improved the watches, so they ran better than originally.

When Henry was 7 years old, it was time to start school. His first day was set for Monday, January 2, 1871, but since the family was snow-bound, the two-mile walk to school had to be delayed until the following Monday.

Mary had already taught him the basics of reading. Henry also excelled at "oral math" and could quickly solve arithmetic problems in his head.

His school was the Scotch Settlement School, a one-room schoolhouse, with a curriculum primarily based on books created by an Ohio schoolmaster, William Holmes McGuffey. The books included a primer, a speller, and four readers. The stories were aimed at kids in rural communities; The speller featured farm tools, such as "A is for Ax," and the readers offered short morality tales with advice such as, "The idle boy is always poor and miserable, but the industrious boy is happy and prosperous." In the fourth reader, students were introduced to classic authors such as Longfellow, Hawthorne, Whittier, Dickens, Scott, Byron, Southey, Wordsworth, and Shakespeare.

Besides educational lessons, the McGuffey Readers dramatized the need for piety, humility, hard work, integrity, patience, kindness, and temperance — all of which fit perfectly with what Henry learned at home.

He loved the readers and took their precepts, with the possible exception of piety, to heart. The long-term impact of the McGuffey Readers on Henry's character and principles was profound and had a significant influence on his life.

Although Henry loved his McGuffey Readers, he still didn't put any more effort into school than was necessary. Basically, he was a bright but unexceptional student with considerably less interest in school than he had in mechanical objects.

He considered school just another chore to try to avoid. He would do what he had to, while he daydreamed about more interesting things. Each day at school was like the day before: After getting the wood stove going, the students read a Bible verse and recited the Lord's Prayer, and the rest of the day was centered around reading, writing, and arithmetic. Whenever possible, the teacher also tried to impress the students with lessons about honor, work, and fair play.

As was typical of the classrooms at that time, the teacher's desk sat on a raised platform at the front of the room. Students were called up to the platform to recite lessons or to write answers on the blackboard. If a student misbehaved, they were required to sit at the front of the class where the teacher could keep an eye on them.

Henry generally managed to stay out of trouble but this doesn't mean he was paying attention. Instead, he was often secretly entertaining himself behind his propped-up geography book, taking apart and reassembling his friends' watches. The teacher was probably aware of this but ignored Henry's subterfuge as long as he was able to get his work done without distracting the rest of the class.

Henry also loved to play pranks on other students. Once during recess, he used his watch tools to bore a couple of small holes in the bottom of the student's seat in front of him. He hid a needle in one hole and ran a string down the other so that when he yanked the string, the needle sprang up to meet the student's unsuspecting posterior. This sudden surprise resulted in a scream and an explosion of giggles from all but one of the students.

In this small schoolhouse, each desk had to be shared by two students. Henry was paired with Edsel Ruddiman, and soon the boys became close friends. They played together every day at recess and after school. They even carved their initials next to each other in their shared desk. Every Sunday, although neither was particularly religious, the two friends walked four miles to church just so they could hang out together.

Henry generally recruited Edsel, as well as other children to assist him with various mechanical projects he would come up with. It always seemed easy for Henry to get his brothers and friends to work for him. Even at an early age, Henry took the lead in devising these ventures and then stepped aside as others implemented them.

For one project, during a lunch break, on a creek near the school, Henry and his friends constructed a dam of stones and mud, with a water wheel driven by the current flowing over their dam. But when the bell rang to leave school at the end of the day, they forgot about their dam, and overnight it ended up flooding the neighboring farmer's potato field.

Another time, Henry led his friends in building a simple turbine engine. They used an old 10-gallon can as the boiler and included a set of tin blades to be spun by the turbine. However, they allowed the boiler to get too hot, and the blades began to spin out of control. Eventually, the boiler exploded, setting fire to a nearby fence. Some of the boys were actually injured by the flying metal, including Henry, who received a lifelong scar on his cheek.

Despite the occasional hazards, Henry's friends loved to follow his lead because he was always filling their playtime with delightful new occupations. And Henry relished in his role as organizer of these projects.

But this idyllic life of friends and adventures suddenly came crashing down. Just as he was about to enter adolescence, a catastrophe struck and devastated his world. On March 29, 1876, Mary was about to give birth to her seventh child. She was in perfect health, and her last six births had been uneventful. But something went wrong, and both mother and newborn died.

This was the most traumatic event of Henry's life. He was only 12 years old, and he couldn't understand how it could have happened or how he could live without his mother. The young boy expressed his pain and inescapable emptiness with a revealing metaphor when he explained, "The house was like a watch without a mainspring."

His mother's death was also the beginning of tensions between Henry and his father. Somehow, the boy seemed to hold his father responsible for the death.

Although Henry had loved his father, his mother had always been the hub of the family and it was to her that he went to for love and understanding. After losing his mother, Henry's feelings toward his father cooled. The fact that they had such different outlooks and personalities was another reason it was difficult to understand each other. Mutual respect still existed, but never the same closeness as when Mary was alive.

Four months after his mother's death, Henry came upon something that launched his life in a new direction. He and his father were on their way to Detroit and about eight miles outside the city they saw a self-propelled wagon coming in the opposite direction. The wagon frame was mounted with a steam engine, and a chain from the engine was driving the rear wheels, so that the wagon moved itself. The driver only had to shovel coal into the fire, manage the throttle, and steer. Henry called this the most noteworthy event of his youth.

He'd seen plenty of these engines being pulled by horses, to be used in locations where they were needed to power threshing machines or sawmills. Even this one wasn't intended as transportation but only as a clever way to get the engine to a thresher. But Henry was astonished because this was the first time he saw a cart move without a horse.

He jumped off his wagon and ran to the steam engine, which had stopped to let them pass, and found the driver more than happy to show off his creation.

It was simply a portable engine and boiler mounted on wheels, pulling a water tank and coal cart behind. The driver explained that the engine made 200 revolutions a minute, and proudly pointed out that the chain pinion could be shifted to let the wagon stop while the engine remained running.

At that moment, several influences in Henry's life came together. His admiration for machines and dislike of manual labor, his mother's example of focusing on efficiency, and even his aversion to horses, were all interwoven in this incredible contraption.

Over the next few years, Henry continued tinkering with watches and machinery while also working on the farm, but everyone in the family knew that Henry would someday leave for the city to learn more about machinery and steam engines. Henry discussed this many times with his father.

The day finally arrived. In 1879, when Henry was 16 years old, he moved into his aunt's boarding house on Baker Street in Detroit. His aunt was Mrs. Rebecca Ford Flaherty, his father's sister. He paid $3.50 per week for room and board.

He quickly found a job at Michigan Car Works (the cars were horse-drawn streetcars) for $1.10 a day. But he was fired after only six days. No one seems to know precisely why; although the reason likely had to do with Henry not being used to having a boss, and with him being more accustomed to giving orders than taking them. It could also be that he made other workers jealous because he loved showing off his skills at fixing machinery.

William would have preferred that his son now return to the farm, but nevertheless, he came to town and helped his son get hired as an apprentice at another machine shop, Flower & Brothers. This was a company owned by James Flower, a good friend of William's.

Perhaps surprisingly, Henry managed to keep this job. At Flower & Brothers, he became friends with Fred Strauss, a 12-year old floor sweeper, who when later asked to describe his friend, responded, "Henry never was a good worker, but he was a good fellow."

Henry wanted to keep this job because Flower & Brothers had a variety of machinery and there was plenty to learn. It was one of the best machine shops in the city, but his pay was only $2.25 for a 60-hour week. He was now earning less than the cost of his room and board.

So, Henry went to see Robert Magill, a jeweler on Michigan Avenue. Henry knew Robert because of the hours he'd spent at the shop looking at watches. Robert agreed to pay Henry $3.00 per week for working six hours per night, six nights a week, making repairs. But he was required to enter by the back door because since he looked young for his age, Robert didn't want his customers to think children were repairing their watches.

Henry enjoyed his job at Flower & Brothers but left after nine months because he felt he'd learned everything they could teach him. This was in the fall, so before looking for another job, he went home to help with the harvest.

After harvesting was complete, he returned to the city and found a job at Detroit Dry Dock Engine Works, a larger operation than Flower & Brothers.

One day at this factory, Henry was pushing a heavy wheelbarrow up a gangplank. The chief engineer, Frank E. Kirby, noticed the struggle and shouted, "Stick in your toenails boy, and you'll make it!" It was a comment Henry remembered and applied throughout his life.

In the fall of 1882, Henry returned to the farm to help again as he did each year. A neighboring farmer, John Gleason, had done well enough to afford a portable steam engine. It wasn't nearly as big as the one that had impressed Henry a half-dozen years earlier, but it was almost as powerful. Although self-propelled, it still wasn't intended for transportation but as a way to get the engine to wherever it could be rented out.

But Gleason didn't understand the machine and in fact was afraid of it. So, he hired Henry to run it for $3 a day. Henry worked all day for the next three months, threshing clover, grinding feed, hauling corn, and sawing wood. It was hard work, and he was exhausted at the end of each day, but he became immensely fond of that machine and became its complete and expert master.

This was Henry's dream job and he was at his absolute happiest when driving that steam engine over the rough country roads at speeds up to 12 miles per hour.

~~~ AUTOMATION ~~~

The automation innovations of Henry Ford launched a manufacturing revolution, which led to a middle-class lifestyle never before dreamed of.

As a young boy, Henry rejected the manual labor that others only thought was their duty to accept. Henry's objection to physical labor on the farm earned him the label of being "lazy." But this was only because others couldn't imagine a life any different. Instead of accepting what was, Henry dreamed of what could be.

Following his mother's many inventive examples, Henry sought and discovered labor saving efficiencies that freed millions from their burdensome labors, and created affordable vehicles that liberated millions from the restraints of distance.

Nikola Tesla

July 10, 1856 – January 7, 1943

The present is theirs; the future, for which I really worked, is mine.
— Nikola Tesla

When Einstein was asked how it felt to be the smartest person alive, his reply was, "I don't know, you'll have to ask Nikola Tesla."

Tesla was a man of dazzling, almost mystical, intellect, but who was also haunted with debilitating obsessions, compulsions, and severe bouts of depression. Within his powerful imagination, Tesla could invent, and in fact, mentally operate and test, entire complex machines without the need of drawings or physical prototypes.

He registered over 300 patents but he also created many more inventions that he never bothered to protect.

Some of the modern technologies reliant on Nikola Tesla's ideas are:

- Ballistics
- Computer science
- Fluorescent lighting
- Lasers
- Nuclear physics
- Radar
- Radio and TV
- Remote control
- Robotics
- Theoretical physics
- X-ray machines

In his second year of college, after a series of upsetting conflicts with a professor over the possibility of an alternating current (AC) motor, Tesla became obsessed with inventing an efficient AC motor.

After his third year of college, Tesla dropped out to concentrate all his attention on solving this puzzle. He felt the answer already existed, "in the deep recesses of the brain." He just needed to find it. He considered this undertaking, "a sacred vow, a matter of life and death."

During the next four years he supported himself working for electrical companies in Budapest and Paris, improving their DC generating stations. All this time, he continued to try out various AC motor designs in his mind.

Then one day, while walking in a park with a friend, the answer suddenly appeared, "like a flash of lightning." He envisioned a motor with no commutators or brushes — no physical contact between the inner and outer cylinders — and in his mind he watched it spinning through the power of electromagnetism.

At the age of 26, after repeated failures trying to interest European investors in his motor, Tesla immigrated to America to work for the great Thomas Edison.

Edison's direct current (DC) equipment was popular but required a generating plant every few blocks. Tesla knew that since AC voltage could be significantly increased with a transformer, it could be delivered to customers much farther away.

But Edison only saw this idea as a threat to his existing DC monopoly. A wide chasm of personalities also separated the two men, and they were poles apart in their inventing styles; Tesla favoring a theoretical approach and Edison preferring trial-and-error experimentation. There was no way for Tesla to change Edison's mind and after six months, he decided to leave.

Two years later he started his own Tesla Electrical company, and over the next decade with the financial backing of George Westinghouse, succeeded in dazzling the public at the Chicago World's fair with 160,000 of his AC lights, and then went on to fulfill his childhood dream of installing AC generators at Niagara Falls.

Just as he had predicted when he was 12 years old, his Niagara Falls generators were capable of sending energy for hundreds of miles, supplying electrical power throughout the entire northeast. With this triumph, Tesla created the foundation of our modern electrical world.

~~~

Thursday morning, July 10, 1856

The darkness of the summer night exploded with lightning, suddenly illuminating the tiny bedroom and overwhelming the yellow glow of the dim gaslight. As the fading thunder crackled outside and the clock chimed midnight, Nikola Tesla was born.

Nikola's parents were Djouka and Milutin Tesla, and Nikola was their fourth child. Nikola's siblings were his 7-year-old brother Dane, and his two sisters: 6-year-old Angelina and 4-year-old Milka. A third sister, Marica, was born three years later.

His father, Milutin came from a family of five children. He was born in Raduč, in the southern part of what is now Croatia, and grew up in Gospić. Milutin's father had been a sergeant in Napoleon's army and later enlisted in the Austrian army.

Milutin attended a German-language public school, then was sent to the Austrian Military Officers' Training, where he and his brother Josif were expected to follow in their father's career. Josif graduated and became an officer, but Milutin had difficulty adapting to military life. Following a rebuke for not properly polishing his brass buttons, Milutin quit and decided to become a priest instead. He enrolled in the Orthodox Seminary in Plaski and graduated in 1845 at the top of his class.

Milutin was passionate about social causes and regularly submitted editorials to the local newspaper under the pen-name Man of Justice. His writings were widely admired for their wit and satire, and they soon attracted the attention of the intellectual elite, one of whom was his future wife, Djouka.

Djouka Mandić was the daughter of a prominent Serbian family and the oldest of seven children. The people in her family were all either priests or married to priests. Her father, Nikola Mandić, was a Serbian Orthodox priest, as was his father before him. Her maternal grandfather, Toma Budesavlievic, was a regal, white-bearded priest, decorated with the French Medal of Honor in 1811 by Napoleon himself.

Djouka was born in the tiny village of Tomingaj, also in the southern part of current-day Croatia. As a child, Djouka had to take on many responsibilities of the home because of her mother's failing eyesight. When Djouka was 16 years old, her mother lost her sight entirely, and Djouka assumed full-time care of the household, including cooking, cleaning, and minding her younger siblings.

Because of her workload, Djouka had no time for formal education and never learned to read. However, she compensated for her illiteracy with her extraordinary memory. She would, in fact, memorize epic Serbian tales, poems, and long Bible passages that were read to her.

Although Milutin's and Djouka's families lived in Croatia — a part of the Austrian Empire — they were Serbian. Austrian authorities encouraged Serbs to settle in their Military Frontier, an area set aside 200 years earlier in the southern part of Croatia as a buffer with the Ottoman Empire, also known as the Turkish Empire or simply Turkey. Immigrants were promised free land and freedom of religion. In exchange, the immigrants, who were already sworn enemies of the Turks (because the Turks had earlier pushed them out of their homeland), were obliged to join the Austrian army to defend the area from Turkish invasion.

Milutin and Djouka were married in 1847 when he was 27, and she was 25; the same year Milutin was ordained as a Serbian Orthodox priest.

The next year, Milutin was assigned a larger parish of 40 households, partly through the help of the Mandić name. Their new home was a stone church atop a high cliff overlooking the Adriatic Sea in the northern coastal fortress of Senj.

Although Milutin enjoyed preaching, his annual salary of 200 forints was hardly enough to feed his family, plus the damp air was affecting his health. Fortunately, after a powerful sermon he delivered on the subject of labor, he was promoted to a congregation of about 80 families in the church of St. Apostles Peter and Paul in the small farming village of Smiljan, located in the province of Lika.

In September 1855, while Djouka was pregnant with Nikola, the couple and their three small children traveled 50 miles by oxcart over the rugged Dinaric Alps to their new home.

The Tesla family's new residence included a small white church, an excellent house for the family, and an allotment of fertile farmland.

Milutin's new congregation was spread over a much larger area, with the nearest members more than two miles away. Soon after he arrived, a Turkish pasha from Bosnia gave Milutin a magnificent Arabian stallion as a reward for assisting some local Muslims. The horse made it easier for Milutin to visit the families throughout his parish.

Nikola's first home was a picturesque agrarian community with an expanse of countryside for exploration and play. It was an ideal environment for young children. Nikola and his siblings ran around the farmyard chasing the pigeons, chickens, geese, and sheep that the family raised. Nikola especially loved watching the birds, wondering how they could fly. In the spring and summer, Nikola and his brother Dane enjoyed the creek, where they went swimming, caught frogs, and in the autumn and early winter, built dams.

Nikola's favorite childhood companion was probably his family's black cat, Mačak. He and the cat liked to "roll and roll" in the grass, and he described the cat as "the fountain of my enjoyment." Mačak followed the boy everywhere, often grabbing him by the trousers. But Mačak was always careful not to hurt him; the instant his needle-sharp incisors penetrated the cloth the pressure would cease.

Nikola — or Niko as his family called him — also liked to watch his mother work. She was an inventive woman, and little Niko was impressed with her mechanical ingenuity. He was fascinated to see her invent devices such as churns, looms, mechanical egg-beaters, and many other labor-saving devices to replace tools that hadn't changed in centuries.

Djouka, a hard-working woman who managed the family's home and farm, typically started work before dawn and usually didn't quit before 11 at night. She was creative and artistic and was well-known for her beautiful needlework; and made most of the clothing and even the furniture in the Tesla home.

Milutin was a stern man and a strict father. Still, Nikola admired how his father ran his life in a precise and orderly fashion. Milutin also had little concern for making any more money than was needed to support his family. He was more interested in social causes and helping humanity.

He was a literate man with a gift for poetry, a published writer, and a serious book collector. He was also known for having a quick wit and a teasing sense of humor. Although Milutin was stern, he was a loving and caring father. He spent time with Nikola with the goal of preparing the boy's mind for the priesthood. The two often studied together. They memorized long romantic poems, repeated complex sentences, performed mental calculations, and sometimes played a game of guessing one another's thoughts.

Nikola's cherished cat, Mačak, also had a rather interesting influence on the boy, for the cat is credited with introducing Nikola to electricity. It happened one dry winter evening when Nikola was 3 years old. He was stroking Mačak's back when he saw an apparent miracle that left him momentarily speechless. The cat appeared to be surrounded by a halo of light, and the motion of the boy's hand produced a shower of sparks that crackled loud enough to be heard throughout the house.

When the cat walked away, the sparks caused it to lift each paw as if it were walking on wet ground.

Nikola asked his parents about what he saw. His mother warned him to stop playing with the cat, or he might start a fire. His father explained that it was only electricity, the same as the lightning in the sky.

The sparks made a deep impression on the young child's imagination. He couldn't stop wondering, "What exactly is this strange force of electricity?"

In 1861, before Nikola was 5 years old, he started attending the Smiljan village primary school, where he studied mathematics, religion, and German. Although he was a bright boy, he was bored with school and easily distracted or lost in thought.

At home, he loved to immerse himself in his father's library. However, instead of supporting his son's curiosity, Milutin was angry when he caught him reading, and especially if it was at night. Milutin believed too much reading at an early age would ruin his son's eyes.

But Nikola was not deterred. He swiped household candles, covered up the keyhole and cracks in his bedroom door, and read until midnight or sometimes until dawn. Not only was he an avid reader, he also discovered that, like his mother, he had an excellent memory.

But it was his older brother Dane that his parents were most proud of. Milutin and Djouka believed their first-born had been gifted to an extraordinary degree, and they felt blessed to have had such a son.

But in 1863, tragedy struck. Dane was riding the family's beloved Arabian horse, when the horse was suddenly spooked and Dane was thrown off, striking his head and dying instantly. Nikolas was nearby and witnessed the accident. Suddenly his 12-year-old brother was gone.

The parents never fully recovered from this devastating loss. In their sorrow, they idealized Dane's talents and grieved for the many remarkable things he might have accomplished. The family sank into sadness, so much so that normal family life was no longer possible.

Although seven years younger, Nikola felt compelled to carry on for Dane by rising to the level of his brother's competence, intelligence, and hopefully, the esteem of his parents.

However, his efforts had the opposite result. Any success or accomplishment of Nikola's seemed dull in comparison to his parents' memory of Dane; if his achievements had any effect, it was to make them feel their loss more keenly.

It's not that his parents didn't love him, but it was impossible to get the attention from them that he now craved. The more Nikola tried to impress his parents, the more he felt rejected, especially by his father, with whom the boy's relationship was now irrevocably diminished.

Milutin's spirit had been permanently crippled. Although he continued his pastoral duties, he wrote fewer articles and embraced fewer causes. He also developed an odd habit of talking to himself, indulging in animated conversations and intense arguments, going so far as adopting different voices so that he sounded like several people. His conduct was so peculiar that neighbors began referring to him as "Old-Man Milutin."

With the loss of his brother and the growing alienation from his parents, Nikola became more introspective and withdrawn. He also adopted several bizarre behaviors. He developed a violent aversion to earrings or pearls on women. He refused to touch another person's hair. He was disturbed by certain smells such as camphor and was even reported to get a fever from just the sight of a peach.

He also acquired many tedious obsessions. He counted his steps as he walked. He couldn't enjoy food unless he first calculated its cubic content. Any repeated acts had to be divisible by three, which meant he was frequently compelled to perform tasks over and over, even if this took hours.

Shortly after Dane's death, the family left their home in Smiljan with the idea of separating themselves from the constant reminders of their lost son. They moved to the nearby town of Gospić, where Milutin began preaching in the sizeable onion-domed Church of the Great Martyr George. Milutin also took a teaching position at the local Real Gymnasium, the equivalent of junior high today.

Gospić was only a few miles from Smiljan, but Nikola was heartbroken to leave his idyllic life on the farm. He had considerable difficulty adjusting to city life and his new school. He felt he didn't fit in with the city boys and had trouble making friends because he couldn't find companions who shared his interests. So, he ended up spending more time at home.

Grief, the relocation, and loneliness weighed heavily on the boy. He had terrifying nightmares, and even after waking, continued to see vivid images of his brother's death and funeral. He was plagued by superstitious beliefs and a constant dread of evil spirits, ghosts, ogres, and other unholy monsters of the dark. To free himself from this torment, he tried to conjure new thoughts and images to push the unwanted thoughts away.

It was during this period that Nikola began experiencing eidetic imagery: mental images so real that they cannot be distinguished from real life. They came unexpectedly and usually appeared when he was in stressful or exhilarating situations.

The visualizations usually began as somewhat blurry images and were sometimes accompanied by annoying flashes of light or the appearance that the air around him was full of flame. Then the images became sharper and so real that he was compelled to reach out to put his hand through them. He sometimes asked one of his sisters whether he was hallucinating or not.

When Nikola was 6, he discovered one way to comfort himself was by accepting his visions and in fact allowing them to develop further. He called these mental adventures his "journeys." During these journeys, he visited imaginary cities and countries where he met people and made friends. He said these friendships felt as dear to him as those in real life, and he returned to them time and again, especially when he was alone at night.

112

School also became an unexpected escape from the visions. Although previously bored with school, the classroom now offered Nikola a break from his mental torture.

One day, in his Gospić elementary school, Nikola saw a model of waterwheels and turbines. He was so fascinated by what he learned that he built several waterwheels of his own in the local stream. When he read about Niagara Falls, he told his Uncle Josif that he wished someday to construct a giant wheel to capture the power of those enormous falls.

Nikola also continued to be captivated by birds and the idea of flight. He once attached four rotors on top of a spindle and tried to fasten June bugs to the blades to cause the blades to rotate. But his experiment was cut short when a boy came by, and to Nikola's disgust, ate his bugs. He abandoned the project and was so unsettled that he could never touch a bug again.

Another of his flight experiments involved grasping a large umbrella and jumping off the roof. Due to the age and condition of the umbrella, it suddenly turned inside-out early in the flight and he spent the next six weeks recovering in bed.

At 7 years old, Nikola came across a novel called *Abafi*, a Serbian translation of a well-known Hungarian writer, Josika. It was the story of a young man who, originally absorbed by debauchery and love of pleasure, used his will power to improve himself and became the most respected hero of his country.

The book inspired Nikola to strengthen his own willpower. Until this time, he had considered his own character to be childish, weak, and vacillating. But this book awakened some incredible powers of determination and self-control. At first, he worked on resisting temptation. If he had a treat he wanted to eat, he gave it to another boy. If he was exhausted by an endeavor, he attacked the task repeatedly until it was done.

After considerable practice, Nikola found he could conquer any feeling and desire. The result was a surprising pleasure at a type of success he had never known: the satisfaction of self-mastery, of being able to do what he willed. He began applying this skill in class. Rather than being uninterested in school, he started enjoying this challenge of pushing his mind to higher and higher achievements.

When Nikola was 10 years old, he entered the Real Gymnasium, where his father and uncle taught. With his newly found strength of will and his ability to see detailed visualizations, he excelled at mathematics and had the ability to rapidly perform complex calculations in his head. Most of his professors were amazed, although some concluded he must be cheating.

After four years at the Real Gymnasium, Nikola moved to Karlovac to attend the Higher Real Gymnasium, the equivalent of high school today, where he studied languages, mathematics, and physics. He boarded with his father's sister, Aunt Stanka, and his uncle, Colonel Brankovic. Karlovac was a town the family had visited many times for vacations. Nikola loved it there, and it was a welcome sanctuary from Gospić city life.

He also enjoyed his new school. He especially liked the classes taught by Professor Martin Sekulic, a physics teacher who made every effort to keep his students abreast of the latest scientific news and discoveries. Professor Sekulic's lab was filled with machine prototypes, many of his own design. Using these physical models, Sekulic not only explained, but could also demonstrate the principles of physics.

One of the more captivating models was a radiometer, an intriguing device invented by British scientist William Crookes. It consisted of four tinfoil vanes resting on a pivot inside a vacuum bulb. Nikola was astonished to see the vanes spin rapidly merely from being exposed to bright light.

In this class, Nikola was introduced to the more mysterious properties of electricity. He was astounded when the professor vigorously cranked the handle of a static electricity machine, and a stream of sparks shot out to contact a small nearby globe of tinfoil.

He read every book he could on electricity and conducted many of his own experiments with batteries, induction coils, water turbines, and motors. He soon realized that he could envision complete experiments in detail before performing them. He began to imagine more complex scenarios, and with discipline and concentration could shape and edit them to mentally test different possibilities.

Nikola recognized that he wasn't like the other boys. He wasn't interested in the same things they were, but he also apparently had abilities others did not. Another thing he discovered was that more than just amusing himself, he could use his abilities to gain approval of the wider world; an acknowledgment he could no longer get at home.

His achievements were now being recognized. He also had mental challenges that exhilarated him. Plus, he was surrounded by the beauty of nature. Life in Karlovac was one of the happiest times for Nikola.

As beautiful as Karlovac was, it lay at the confluence of four rivers and was a marshy area plagued by mosquitoes. After a day of exploring during his last year there, Nikola developed a fever, which turned out to be malaria. He was seriously ill for several days, and in fact, even after recovering, the disease continued to rack his body with aches and fever for at least three more years.

While he was recuperating and being treated with substantial amounts of quinine, the local library sent him their uncatalogued books which he agreed to read and classify. Among them were several recent novels by Mark Twain, which he found so captivating that he claimed they made him forget his illness.

By 1873, 17-year-old Nikola had completed the four-year high school in three years. It was time to move back to Gospić, and he decided that he must now tell his father that he was passionate about science and mathematics, and that he wished to pursue engineering instead of becoming a priest. But Milutin wouldn't budge and was still determined that his son follow him into the priesthood.

There was little time to convince his father because shortly after returning home, he once again fell seriously ill. Gospić was in the grip of a cholera epidemic, and probably due to Nikola's still weakened condition, he was soon stricken. This time, he was bed-ridden for nine months. He continued to deteriorate until it seemed there was no hope. His family was so convinced of his imminent death that his coffin was ordered.

Milutin's father came to Nikola's bedside and pleaded with his son not to give up. He had already lost one son and couldn't lose another. Milutin told Nikola that if he survived, he would send him to the best engineering institution there was. It was a gesture of desperation because no one survived past this point of the illness.

But, to everyone's amazement, and possibly from the inspiration of his father's promise, or else from the administration of an herbal cure, Nikola did recover. And his father kept his word. For Nikola's engineering training, they chose the Polytechnic School, in Graz, Austria, 175 miles to the north.

However, Nikola first needed to serve three years in the army. A major war was breaking out against the Turks, and Milutin knew his son would never be a successful soldier. He was sure that military enlistment would be a death sentence for his son. Although avoiding conscription was a serious offense, Milutin asked his son to go into hiding while Milutin looked for a way to prevent Nikola from going to war.

For the next nine months, from early fall until summer, Nikola roamed the mountains of Croatia with only a hunter's outfit and a bundle of books. This extended contact with nature had the effect of strengthening him in mind, as well as body. He discovered a new capacity for being alone and used this solitary time to further develop his peculiar thinking and visualizing skills.

While he hiked in the mountains, he came up with many ideas. Most of these were impractical schemes that he was later forced to abandon. But while building these fanciful inventions, Nikola was delighted to discover that he could produce even the most complex devices entirely in his imagination with no need to sketch them.

He also found that while working on these mental models, he could explore the underlying concepts involved. For Orthodox Christians, everything in the universe has an underlying ideal. Although Nikola doesn't appear to have practiced his faith, he apparently absorbed an interest in seeking the underlying conceptual principles that his ideas were based on.

As he continued to practice, Nikola discovered that it was essential to find a balance between letting his imagination run freely, enforcing enough discipline to work out details, and validate the basic concept behind the ideas.

During Nikola's exile, Milutin negotiated with the government and finally arranged for Nikola to attend the Polytechnic School on a Military Frontier scholarship. The scholarship paid 420 guldens a year for three years, at the end of which Nikola must agree to eight years of military service.

Nikola was a grown man now; at 19 years old, he was 6 feet 2 inches tall with deep-set light blue eyes, angular facial features, high cheekbones, and uncommonly long fingers. He arrived for his first day at the Austrian Polytechnic school with his hair combed back, and wearing a fine suit and hat, plus white gloves to avoid hand contact.

In college, Nikola was in his element. He had his mother's work ethic and creativity and his father's commitment and organization skills, and he was driven by his overwhelming desire to discover and create new things.

Not only was he a naturally brilliant student, but he worked hard at his studies, starting every day at 3 in the morning, and not sleeping until 11 at night. During his first year, he never missed a lecture, made the highest possible grades, and started a Serb cultural club. The dean even sent a letter of commendation to his father, saying, "Your son is a star of the first rank."

Unbeknownst to Nikola, his father also received another letter, warning that unless he removed his son from school, Nikola would likely kill himself from overwork.

As much as Nikola reveled in engineering, he soon became caught up in an ongoing dispute with one of his professors over the requirement of commutators in electric motors. Professor Poeschl mocked and ridiculed Nikola's ideas, which caused Nikola's obsessive compulsions to flare up, forcing him to repeatedly excuse himself from class to wash his hands.

The disagreement was about something that would become Nikola's life's work. It started one day during his second year at school when he was 20 years old.

Professor Poeschl was showing the Gramme dynamo prototype of a direct current system. Nikola was impressed with the demonstration but thought the associated sparking of the commutator was dangerous and a waste of energy. "Can anything be done with that annoying discharge?" he asked.

"It is direct current, and we haven't found a way to avoid it," his teacher answered. "It seems inherent in the nature of the machine. It may be reduced to a great extent, but as long as we use commutators, it will always be present." He went on to explain, "Since a magnet has two poles, each of which acts oppositely, we will have to use a commutator to change at the right moment, the directions of the current in the rotating armature."

Nikola responded, "That is obvious. The machine is limited by the type of current used. I am suggesting that we get rid of the commutators entirely by using alternating current!"

~~~ SCIENTIST ~~~

Nikola Tesla was a scientist of mythical proportions. He had attained unimaginable levels of focus and concentration, but within this same extraordinary mind, lurked anguishing levels of psychological pain. We can't know for sure, but his exceptional mental abilities may have arisen from his attempts to cope with those debilitating mental demons.

As a child, he was a loner and found it difficult to make close friends, and after the death of his brother, it also became difficult for him to be close with his parents. His lifelong desire to fascinate the public with amazing scientific demonstrations may have been an attempt to fill this void.

Like his father, Tesla primarily focused on the betterment of mankind. Like his mother he was consumed with devising new and better ways to do things. He succeeded at both and the world still remains fascinated by this extraordinary person... and grateful for the scientific advances he gave us.

Thomas Edison

February 11, 1847 – October 18, 1931

The most certain way to succeed is to try just one more time.
— Thomas Edison

In 1877, Thomas Alva Edison's invention of the phonograph made the 30-year-old the most famous person in the world. It also marked the end of history's silence, for we are deaf to all sounds and voices preceding this invention.

Thomas Edison patented more than 1,000 inventions and established entirely new industries, including electric lights, power stations, sound recording, and motion pictures, all of which dramatically changed the way we live.

Known as "The Wizard of Menlo Park," Edison developed what was basically an invention factory, where he would identify a specific need and then put teams of engineers to work on finding a solution, usually through exhaustive experimentation.

After his invention of the phonograph, Edison immediately went to work on developing a long-lasting and safe incandescent lightbulb. This invention required over a year of experimenting with more than 1,000 types of filaments, until his final success in 1879 at last freed mankind from the nightly constraints of the dark.

To run these lights and his many other electrical inventions, he opened the first commercial power station in New York City in September 1882 and for the first time, homes and businesses had access to the magical power of electricity.

Thomas Edison was a celebrity during his time and is still idolized today for his brilliance and tenacity. For many people, Thomas Edison is the first name that comes to mind when they think of the word "inventor." In fact, the very icon for the word "idea" is an image of a lightbulb over the head.

Edison wasn't only a prolific inventor. He was also an ingenious marketer. He promoted himself as a brand as persistently as he promoted his products. Soon, practically every household had at least one of his devices, each of which was boldly emblazoned with the name EDISON.

All these products started with the one invention which would always remain his favorite: the phonograph. This stunning and world-changing innovation was the beginning of this man's remarkable career. But what was the beginning of this exceptionally prodigious inventor?

~~~

Thursday, February 11, 1847

It was 3 a.m. and the freezing wind howling off nearby Lake Erie was piling towering snow drifts against the front of the small house. In a tiny back bedroom, Dr. Lehman Galpin, a friend and neighbor, placed the newborn in its mother's arms.

Nancy and Samuel Edison stared anxiously at their baby boy, studying him in the light of the flickering oil lamp. The baby was fair with gray eyes and looked the very image of his mother. The couple had lost two sons – 6-year-old Carlile Snow and 3-year-old Samuel Ogden, III – only one year earlier. These painful memories, and the high infant mortality rate in the mid-nineteenth century, led to a careful and apprehensive examination of their new son.

Thomas Alva Edison looked fine in all regards, except he had an unusually big forehead. Dr. Galpin explained that although the baby's head was larger than usual, it looked well-shaped and normal. But he added that it was still possible the child might have "brain fever," or inflammation of the brain, so the parents should watch for any other symptoms such as fevers or rashes.

The baby was named Thomas after his father's older brother in Canada, and Alva after his father's good friend in Milan, Captain Alva Bradley. As a young boy, Thomas Alva Edison was usually called Al.

The family lived in the small town of Milan, Ohio, three miles off the southwest shore of Lake Erie, in a simple brick cottage the father had constructed five years earlier. It was a plain one-story house built on a hillside so that its basement opened onto the rear yard. The house was heated by a fireplace with an open coal grate that wasn't always adequate in severe winters.

Thomas Edisons' Birthplace

Thomas's ancestors on his father's side were of Dutch descent and immigrated to New Jersey, where they lived until their loyalty to the British drove them to Nova Scotia, Canada during the American Revolution.

Two generations later, on August 16, 1804, Samuel Edison was born in Digby, Nova Scotia.

Nancy Mathews Elliot's ancestors came from Scotland and lived in Chenango County, New York, where Nancy was born on January 4, 1810.

When she was a teenager, her family moved to Vienna, Ontario, where Nancy was working as a teacher when she met Samuel, a local hotel manager.

Samuel and Nancy married on September 12, 1828, when he was 24 years old, and she was 18. They stayed in Vienna for the first nine years of their marriage, and this is where their first four children — Marion, William, Harriett, and Carlile – were born.

Samuel had a keen interest in politics, especially in the writings of the American philosopher Thomas Paine. So, it was no surprise when in December 1837, Samuel joined the Mackenzie Rebellion in Toronto, objecting to "taxation without representation." Having learned their lesson the last time, the British immediately quashed this new rebellion with overwhelming force, arresting and hanging nine members of Samuel's Vienna brigade for treason.

Samuel escaped and traveled west on foot for three days through snow-covered forests. He crossed the frozen St. Clair River to enter the U.S. at Port Huron, Michigan, then continued south until he reached Milan, Ohio.

In Milan, Samuel made the acquaintance of Captain Alva Bradley, a shipowner from Vermilion, Ohio, who sympathized with Samuel's plight. Bradley sailed across Lake Erie to Canada and rescued Nancy and the four children, and brought the family back to Milan. Captain Bradley then loaned Samuel enough money to start a shingle mill in Milan.

The town of Milan was connected by a wide canal to the Huron River, which emptied into Lake Erie. On the path along this waterway, mules hauled 250-ton barges of grain. Vast quantities of grain were grown in the area, and after the canal was built, the grain could reach customers in New York and beyond. In fact, Milan had become one of the leading grain ports of the world, second only to the Russian city of Odessa.

It was a promising location to start a business and before long Samuel had plenty of demand for his shingles and was soon employing several men at his mill.

When Thomas was born, he had four siblings: 17-year-old Marion Wallace, 15-year-old William Pitt, 13-year-old Harriet Ann "Tannie," and 2-year-old Eliza Smith.

Samuel and Nancy were never confident about Thomas's health because he was a sickly child with a fragile appearance. But they were comforted by the fact that he was usually a contented baby and rarely cried.

However, barely a year after Thomas was born, his sister Eliza died at 3½ years old. After losing three children in quick succession, Nancy Edison became fiercely protective toward her youngest child.

Nancy was 37 when Thomas was born, but she still looked like the bright, pretty teacher Samuel had married 19 years earlier. She no longer taught school though because at the time, women were required to retire from teaching when they married.

Thomas's father was a robust man of 42 years, 6-feet tall with blue-gray eyes and silver hair and beard. And because of Samuel's thriving business and outgoing nature, the Edisons were a prominent family in their small town.

Thomas's early childhood memories were scant, but one scene always stuck with him. He remembered chasing a shiny silver coin that Homer Page, a prosperous neighboring farmer, rolled across their locust-wood floor. The following year Mr. Page became Thomas's brother-in-law when he married his oldest sister, Marion.

Another memory from a couple of years later was of the long wagon trains passing through town on their way to California. Each of these brightly painted, canvas-covered wagons carried whole families with all their worldly belongings. The wagons were traveling thousands of miles along the California Trail through vast open spaces and dangerous Indian country, chasing visions of striking it rich in the great California Gold Rush, which had started the year after Thomas was born. Witnessing this migration was his first impression of a larger world that existed beyond his home.

Thomas's brother and sisters were too much older to be playmates. To the young boy, they were more like other adults in the house, and he was essentially raised as an only child by a houseful of parents.

Although his brother William was too old to play with, Thomas loved watching him sketch, which is how William spent most of his free time. He was also impressed with the passion his sister Tannie had for writing and with the stacks of journals she filled with her notes and compositions.

Thomas spent most of his time playing alone, which may be part of the reason he was a late speaker, not beginning to talk until almost his fourth birthday.

As soon as he started talking though, he started asking questions. The boy pleaded with every adult to explain the workings of everything he saw. If they said they didn't know, he stared at them with his deep-set eyes, and asked, "Why?" His constant interruptions were so frustrating to the mill workers that one of Mr. Edison's workers joked to Samuel that the mill could save money if they hired a man just to answer the boy's questions.

Even Samuel said that Thomas's questions sometimes exhausted him. However, Samuel didn't consider these constant queries to be from curiosity, but simply from dullness. After all, other kids didn't constantly need everything explained to them.

According to Samuel, his son never had a boyhood in the ordinary sense. Most of Thomas's early childhood was spent in rather odd and solitary occupations. One favorite pastime was building little plank roads out of debris from the shingle mill. One time he was seen in the village square laboriously copying all the store signs. Another time, his sister discovered him sitting on a nest he had built, trying to hatch goose eggs he'd collected from the barn.

His eagerness to explore and experiment meant he always needed to be watched closely. Once, leaning too close to the canal, he fell in and was only rescued because an observant bystander happened to be nearby. Another time, he climbed and fell into a tall grain elevator and nearly drowned in the wheat, but fortunately again, someone saw the boy and just in time was able to pull him out. He wasn't always so lucky though and lost the tip of a finger while holding a skate strap for another boy to shorten with an ax.

One day, this curious boy created a disaster that caught the attention of the entire community. He wanted to find out how different types of wood might burn, but the wood was close to some hay, and a fire quickly engulfed the entire barn. Several neighbors rushed to contain the blaze before it could spread. Once the fire was out, Samuel gave the boy a public spanking in the village square.

Clearly, the young boy needed constant supervision. Even his adoring mother was occasionally forced to get the switch from behind the Seth Thomas grandfather clock: once for breaking open a bumblebee's nest to see what was inside, another time for feeding a young neighbor girl "bird food" of mashed worms to see if it would make her fly.

He was troublesome and inquisitive but Nancy refused to believe her son was stupid and pointed to examples of his extraordinarily retentive memory. For instance, before he was 5 years old, he knew all the songs the lumber gangs and canal men sang.

In 1854, when Thomas was 7 years old, the Edisons had to leave Milan. Twenty-five years earlier, the town had invested tens of thousands of dollars in their canal, and they now had disdain for the new railroad promoters who they only saw as competition. The town fathers turned down an offer by the Lake Shore Railroad to build a station there, but then the area farmers abandoned the canal, and carted their crops to a neighboring town where they could ship by rail.

The Edisons sold their home for little money and moved 100 miles north to the city of Port Huron, Michigan. Thomas didn't want to leave and was even more disturbed when he found that his sister Marion and his "Uncle" Homer wouldn't be joining them, and instead were staying behind on their farm.

On a beautiful spring day, the Edisons left Milan for good. As sad as it was for Thomas, it was also an unforgettable adventure to travel so far from home through the pristine forests and to witness new sights, such as the many Indians paddling their canoes on Lake St. Clair.

Arriving in Port Huron, the Edison's found a vibrant lumber town with many busy sawmills. They rented a large, two-story Colonial house on 10 acres at the edge of town overlooking the St. Clair River. The property included a carriage house, barn, icehouse, and woodshed. The house had an oven in the kitchen fireplace and six bedrooms upstairs, which Mrs. Edison used to supplement the family's income by taking in boarders.

Samuel went to work selling timber, growing vegetables, and running a small grocery store. William became a partner in a livery stable and moved into a small house next to it. Although the Edisons weren't rich, they were living comfortably.

The next year, Samuel began one of his most remarkable enterprises. He built a 100-foot-tall wooden tower in a clearing between the trees behind their house. At the top of the winding stairs, he added an observation platform and a telescope. For 25 cents and a long climb, a visitor could enjoy a beautiful aerial view of the surrounding forests and river.

For the first two months, the tower took in only $3. Many neighbors began mocking what they called the "Edison Tower," and it seemed the family might be the only ones who would appreciate the panorama.

However, the railroad began promoting the tower as a destination excursion, and the Edisons started to earn more each year than the tower had cost to build. One day, 600 people showed up to picnic in the grove and hike to the top of the tower. Eight-year-old Thomas collected the admission fee from the visitors and was overwhelmed by the impressive pile of coins. It was astonishing how many people were willing to pay you if you made something they liked.

Thomas continued to suffer with health issues, including a severe case of Scarlet Fever, which resulted in ear infections that damaged his hearing and left him with hearing loss that worsened over the years.

Because of his constant health struggles, Thomas didn't start school until he was 8 years old. As was common at the time, this was in a private, church-run, one-room schoolhouse.

He was a challenging student who questioned everything, and then he often disagreed with the answers he received. He also had trouble paying attention. Possibly, he suffered from attention deficit disorder, or perhaps he just struggled with poor hearing.

Regardless of the reason, his teacher, the Reverend G. B. Engle, was exasperated and concluded that Thomas must have some type of mental illness. He explained to Mary that the boy's inabilities may have to do with his misshapened head, and concluded by saying that, in his opinion, Nancy's son was "addled" and would never be able to learn.

Thomas cried when he heard this because he thought the teacher was probably right. He was always at the "foot of the class," had difficulty with words and speech, and couldn't learn arithmetic. His father was also concerned about what he figured was his son's stupidity.

But Mrs. Edison would have none of this. She realized from her pedagogic experience that her son was receptive and observant, and she thought his atypical demeanor and physical appearance were outward signs of a remarkable intelligence.

She was so indignant about the teacher's assessment that after only 12 weeks of class she pulled her son from school. Nancy was eager to teach Thomas at home and was confident she could give him a better education than the school.

Under Nancy's regime of patient teaching and commitment to nurturing his curiosity, Thomas experienced a complete and rapid turnaround. He now felt he had a reason to learn: someone who believed in him and whom he wouldn't want to disappoint.

Nancy taught Thomas to read, write, and sketch. Samuel encouraged his reading with a 10-cent bribe for every novel or history book he completed. It wasn't long though before Thomas was eager to read without prompting. He became an aggressive learner and read voraciously, with a particular fondness for history, English literature, and poetry.

By the time Thomas was 10, his parents had taught him all they could, and the young boy began learning on his own. He worked his way through the family's extensive library paying particular attention to classic novels and popular science periodicals.

Thomas developed a highly individualistic, analytical, and skeptical style of learning. He questioned prevailing theories and accepted nothing unless he could test it firsthand. This "addled" child turned into a serious-minded scholar: curious, competitive, dexterous, meticulous, and enthusiastic. He was also likely driven to prove the Reverend Engle wrong.

Since he wasn't at school, he had time for other occupations and soon began a business to earn some money on his own. He and his closest companion, Michael Oates — a Dutch lad several years older than Thomas who worked for the Edisons doing chores around the house — began growing vegetables on part of the family's 10 acres. Thomas and Michael sowed and reaped, and then went door-to-door selling corn, radishes, onions, parsnips, and beets. They split the income, and Thomas, still 10 years old, handed his half over to his mother for safe-keeping. In just one year, he earned $600, the equivalent of $16,000 today!

At 11 years old, from the books he was reading, Thomas developed an interest in chemistry and outfitted the first of his many laboratories in the family's cellar. He got a copy of Parker's School Philosophy, an elementary book on physics, and planned on trying every experiment in the book.

He collected over 200 bottles from various places around town and arranged them on shelves, all with the label "Poison" so they wouldn't be disturbed. He spent some of his vegetable income on filling the bottles with chemicals he bought from local drug stores. Thomas was soon familiar with all these chemicals because he wouldn't believe anything he read in his books until he had tested it himself.

Eventually, his mother became concerned about the clutter and possible results of these strange experiments, and she ordered Thomas to clear this mess out of her house. But her son was distraught at the thought of losing his laboratory, and of course, Mary finally relented, insisting that he at least put a lock on the door so that only he had access to the eyesore.

Thomas was now spending most of his spare time in the cellar. He had no interest in sports or the other activities of the boys in his neighborhood. He either worked alone in his laboratory or enlisted Michael Oates as his assistant.

When he wasn't running experiments in his laboratory, Thomas was continuing his self-education. When he outgrew the family library, his parents taught him how to use the town's public library, and he was spellbound to discover this vast store of free information. As was characteristic of his "frontal attack" approach, he systematically set out to read every book, a shelf at a time.

His parents though guided him to be a bit more selective. By the time he turned 12, he'd completed Gibbon's *Rise and Fall of The Roman Empire*, Hume's *History of England*, Sears' *History of The World*, and Burton's *Anatomy of Melancholy*. He also devoured *The World Dictionary of Science* and several works on practical chemistry. This was no small feat for a young boy, but Thomas had an extraordinary sense of perseverance.

He also struggled through Newton's *Principia* but was disillusioned by the classical aristocratic terms, which he thought were unnecessarily confusing. The mathematics of *Principia* were also beyond Thomas's grasp, but he never was much of a mathematician.

However, he was attracted to the beauty of Newton's physical laws. He was also inspired by Newton's methods of objective examination and experimentation, which caused him to sharpen his own freewheeling experiments by employing a more deliberate approach of planning and testing specific hypotheses.

His chemical experiments also led to a familiarity with the nature of electric batteries and their currents. This introduced Thomas to a new realm of experimentation because just as with chemistry, he would not accept anything about electricity without thoroughly testing it.

When Thomas was 12 years old, he asked his parents if he could take a job selling newspapers on the train that ran through Port Huron. For a boy who wasn't in regular attendance at school, this was an opportunity to make the money he needed to support his increasingly expensive chemistry lab, plus the chance to read all the newspapers and magazines for free.

Although the Edison's weren't poor, supporting the family was an ongoing struggle, so Thomas's interest in getting a job may have been inspired by listening to his parents discussing their finances. Whatever his motivation, it's clear that his earliest ambitions typically involved making money.

At first, his parents, particularly his mother, were opposed to him working on the train. But with persistence, Thomas persuaded them to let him apply for the job, and by the winter of 1859, he was a "news butcher" on the Grand Trunk Railroad Line. In this job, he walked up and down the aisles selling peanuts, candy, and newspapers to passengers. He boarded the train each morning at 7 and returned to Port Huron at 9:30 in the evening.

The 63-mile trip to Detroit, Michigan, took three hours, and he had to wait in Detroit for eight hours before getting on the train for the journey home. The downtime in Detroit wasn't wasted though, because the city had an extensive library, where he found plenty of technical books to read.

Thomas was provided his own area on the train for his inventory. The train's baggage car was divided into three compartments: one for trunks and packages, one for mail, and one for smoking. As there was no ventilation, the smoking compartment was never used, so this space was turned over to Thomas for his stock of goods.

It soon also became his laboratory. After his mother complained again about the smells and dangers in her cellar, he transferred much of his equipment and chemicals to the smoking-car. Now he could conduct his scientific experiments during any spare time on the train.

To have more time available for experimenting, Thomas hired other boys to do his selling for a share of the profits. He then added vegetables, butter, and seasonal berries to his merchandise. As business grew, he assigned boys to other trains and also set up stores in the train stations. To grow his business, he added fresh fruits, cheese, dairy products, and dry goods that he bought from farmers along the way, plus delicacies from Detroit.

Thomas now had time to run his rolling chemistry lab and was making an excellent income: $8 to $10 daily, or around $250 in today's money.

A few months later, Thomas added to his income again by opening two stores in his hometown of Port Huron, so his neighbors could save the trip to Detroit for groceries.

Even though his train stockroom was always full, surprisingly Thomas was never asked to pay for freight. He assumed they left him alone because he was so small and industrious and had the nerve to appropriate a U.S. mail car. But the fact that he gave the wives of conductors, engineers, and other trainmen the benefit of a wholesale discount may have also played a part in his exemption.

Thomas continued to branch out whenever he saw an opportunity. When his hero, Abraham Lincoln, was nominated on May 18, 1860, he distributed campaign literature and sold flattering photographs of Lincoln.

During this time, the hearing loss he suffered when he was 8 continued to worsen. By the time Thomas was 14, it had deteriorated to the point that he was totally deaf in his left ear and had 80 percent loss in his right. Reading was now the only way he could learn; it would have been impossible to attend a typical school.

But Thomas seemed to have a natural inclination for accepting fate. When things were beyond his control, he adapted, compensated, and developed alternative methods. He was also too busy to think about disabilities.

When the War of Rebellion broke out on April 12, 1861, Thomas noticed an increased demand for newspapers, so he decided to publish his own. He bought a second-hand printing press that had been used for hotel bills of fare and got some old type for free from friends at the Detroit Free Press.

It wasn't long before Thomas learned the basics of printing and added a publishing business to the smoking-compartment that was already crowded with newspapers, produce, jars of chemicals, and test tubes. He became the compositor, pressman, editor, publisher, and news-dealer of the weekly Grand Trunk Herald. The price was 3 cents a copy, or 8 cents a month.

He hired another friend to assist with this new enterprise, and because of the demand for news of the war, his single-sided, two-sheet paper added another $10 to his daily income.

In the beginning, The Herald mostly ran stories about the train's officers, trainmen, station agents, telegraph operators, and trackmen. The printing wasn't always perfect, and neither was the spelling or punctuation, but passengers enjoyed it because he printed news of local importance that the distant papers in Detroit couldn't get. His business did so well that no less than the London Times made mention of the "first newspaper in the world to be printed on a train in motion."

One day while the cars were being shunted, Thomas was standing on the platform and noticed a small boy wandering onto the main track just as a car without a brakeman was rapidly approaching. Thomas dropped his stack of papers and ran to the track, and barely in time, was able to grab the child.

The little boy's father, station agent J. U. Mackenzie, saw this and was so relieved, that he offered to show his gratitude by teaching Thomas to be a telegraph operator. Telegraphy was the high-tech skill at that time, so this was like offering to teach computers and programming to a young boy today.

The offer was eagerly accepted, and Thomas began mastering the dots and dashes of Morse Code. At a gun-shop in Detroit, he built his own set of instruments to practice with. Then he turned part of his newsboy duties over to a friend and spent the next few months pursuing this new course of study.

He and a neighbor boy set up a telegraph line between their houses, running stove-pipe wires between trees, and using glass bottles as insulators. The friends exchanged messages until late each night. Thomas began to sleep fewer and fewer hours as he split his time between chemistry, his various businesses, and now telegraphy.

In April 1862, Thomas noticed the bulletin boards outside the Detroit newspaper were surrounded by throngs of people anxious for any news about the Battle of Shiloh, a battle in which Grant and Sherman were engaged. Confederate General Johnson had been killed, and the two sides suffered a staggering 60,000 casualties.

He decided that if he found the same excitement at the other stations, instead of the usual 100 papers, he could probably sell 1,000!

He approached the operator in the Detroit depot and gave him a three-month subscription to Harper's Weekly and some other papers in exchange for telegraphing the stations down the line and asking them to chalk the breaking headlines on their train schedule boards.

He then walked into the Detroit Free Press, and in desperation, asked to speak to the editor about some "important business." He was led to an office where he explained to two men what he had done with telegraphed headlines, and said he wanted a thousand papers, but on credit, because he could only afford 300.

One man laughed and said that would be impossible, but the other, Wilbur F. Storey (who later went on to found the Chicago Times), told the first man to go ahead and let the boy have the papers.

The first stop with this larger inventory was Utica, which was a small station where he usually sold about two papers. But this time he sold 35. He decided that if he found a similar crowd at the next station, the only thing to do was to raise the price to 10 cents. After that, he continued to sell papers at ever-increasing rates. By the time he got to Port Huron, he jumped off the train and yelled, "Twenty-five cents apiece, gentlemen! I don't have enough to go around!"

He quickly sold the rest of his papers and ended the day with quite a large sum of money. It was a stunning lesson to Thomas that people were willing to pay almost any price to get something when they really wanted it. But as much money as he was making, he was spending it just as quickly on new supplies and costly chemicals.

To handle the growing congestion in his train car, he had wooden shelves built to hold his chemicals on the walls. But one day the train hit an uneven piece of track at 30 miles per hour, and the sudden lurch sent a stick of phosphorus crashing to the floor, where it burst into flames. Thomas was trying to stomp out the fire when the conductor, a quick-tempered Scotsman, rushed in with a bucket of water to drench the flames.

The next stop was Mount Clemens, where Thomas, his laboratory, and his printing press were thrown off the train, and he was told he could now only sell his papers from the stations.

His laboratory was moved back into his mother's cellar. He continued his publishing but changed the nature of his paper. He renamed it to *Paul Pry* and turned it into more of a general interest paper, plus made it decidedly more personal and gossipy, freely expressing his opinions of people and events.

The paper wasn't universally popular, and one unappreciative victim of his attention found Thomas one day and tossed him into the St. Clair River. This assault on the press must have dampened the young editor's enthusiasm for journalism because soon after that, he gave up the business.

Because he was well acquainted with the operators along the railroad, Thomas was soon recommended to a Mr. M. Walker who owned a jewelry store that also sold his own newspapers and periodicals. Mr. Walker gave Thomas a job copying press reports that came over the wires each night until 3 a.m.

With this experience, plus a recommendation from Mr. Mackenzie, the 16-year-old Thomas next applied for a night-operator job at the Stratford Junction in Ontario, Canada.

His parents agreed to let him go since Stratford wasn't far — less than 100 miles from Port Huron — and their son would be close to Bayfield, where the Edisons had friends and relatives.

Thomas began this new job in the late spring of 1863. The Stratford station wasn't busy, so Thomas spent much of his time reading and studying chemistry. He would frequently find an interesting article in papers such as the Scientific American, and then disappear, not to be seen again until his new experiment was completed.

The Stratford Station was where Thomas developed his first mechanical "invention." Night operators worked from 7 p.m. until 7 a.m. This suited Thomas because it left his daytime free for experimenting ... that is, if he wasn't too tired. To prove they were awake, each hour the operators had to telegraph the signal "6," a practice known as "sixing," to the dispatcher's office. To get around this inconvenience, Thomas constructed a small wheel with notches on the rim and attached it to a clock, so that each hour, the wheel automatically transmitted the required "dah-di-di-di-dit," leaving Thomas free to nap in his chair.

Another indication of his growing inventiveness occurred that winter during a visit home to Port Huron. An ice jam had broken the telegraph cable that lay across the bottom of the three-quarter mile wide river and interrupted essential railway communications. Thomas saved the day by suggesting they use the steam whistle of the locomotive to relay the signals across the river.

Although Thomas was a good operator and a fast learner, a near disaster ended his job in Stratford. One day, he was ordered to stop a train that was on a collision course with an oncoming train. The train was faster than he had expected, and it passed before he could flag it down.

Fortunately, the engineers of the two trains spotted each other and were able to stop in time, but Thomas was threatened with arrest for criminal negligence. Mr. Mackenzie was left with the awkward task of explaining why a 16-year-old boy had been entrusted with such an important job. Thomas didn't wait to find if he would be arrested; he boarded the next train out of town.

Returning to the U.S., he decided to join the growing ranks of freelance telegraph operators. The military had taken many operators, so there was a strong demand for those who were willing to relocate as needed.

Unlike Europe, where the telegraph systems were managed by the government, anyone in America was free to enter the field. Many young, unmarried men soon jumped at the opportunity to roam the country working for the highest bidder.

This type of job attracted a rowdy group of people, who although well paid, typically consumed much of their easy money on liquor. Thomas had a tobacco habit but never drank, and this one attribute set him apart in the eyes of many potential employers.

While other "tramp operators" were carousing, Thomas continued his self-education and experiments. He took his telegraphy profession seriously and constantly looked for ways to improve his performance. One example was timed tests of different writing methods to discover which was quickest. From these experiments, he settled on vertical print, rather than the more usual cursive, as the fastest way to copy messages, a method which later became the industry standard.

Thomas also practiced increasing his reading speed and got so expert that he could sense the meaning of a whole line of text at once. He wondered why this wasn't taught in school because he found it to be an easily acquired skill. Now he could read two or three books a day, whereas if he looked at each word, his reading was laborious and much slower.

During this time, Thomas kept a notebook of technical drawings and spent time in local libraries reading every book on electricity he could find. He got a chance to explore many libraries because his job kept him on the move.

In August 1866, Thomas and two of his operator friends traveled down to New Orleans, with plans to go to Brazil. With the war over and a flood of returning operators, there were many advertisements from South American companies offering good jobs, a comfortable life, and a low cost of living.

Thomas and his friends explained their intentions to an old South American gentleman sitting by the steamer agent's desk. The man emphatically told them it would be the worst mistake of their lives. The old man shook his yellow bony finger and warned that they would regret forsaking their native land, whose freedom, climate, and opportunities could not be equaled anywhere in the world.

Thomas took the old man's advice and remained in the U.S., taking a new job in Boston, Massachusetts. His two friends continued to Vera Cruz, Mexico, where Thomas later learned they died of yellow fever.

For Thomas, Boston was the most exciting place a telegraph operator could be. Boston at this time was to telegraph technology as Silicon Valley would be to computers a century later. With the glut of operators recently mustered from the military, it was becoming an increasingly competitive field. Operators there, held regular meetings to discuss new developments and compete for speed and accuracy.

Thomas found that as fast as he could write, it still wasn't always possible for him to keep up with the transmission speeds, and it was sometimes necessary to fill in the blanks with guesses.

To remedy this, Thomas designed and built another invention: a device to record the dots and dashes with indentations on a rotating disk of paper, the line of indents forming a continuous spiral as the disk turned. He was then able to transcribe the message more accurately by slowing the disk and playing back his "recording."

~~~ INVENTOR ~~~

It's difficult to overestimate the impact of this one inventor, not only because of his inventions, but through his influence on the process of inventing itself, turning it from serendipitous discovery to a deliberate and purposeful search for solutions to recognized problems.

As a child, it wasn't initially obvious what he would become. A late-speaking, loner, with an odd-shaped head, and non-stop questions, who was labeled "addled" by his teacher (and stupid by his father); managed through the confidence and support of his mother, a retired teacher, to grow into history's most preeminent inventor.

Suffering with a serious hearing impairment, and possibly with attention deficit disorder, this young man exercised an uncommon grit and determination to forge his character into one of self-confidence and tenacity to become a world-wide hero and a permanent icon of history.

Observations

You've probably come across a number of discoveries and surprises as you read these stories. Each reader will see these stories from their individual perspective, but I've left my own thoughts to the end of the book so as not to bias your observations.

These children certainly had plenty in common. In fact, it's tricky to remember which episode went with which biography because they shared several similar experiences.

But there are aspects of their lives which also make them stand out as unique individuals. Although as children, they were naturally childish in many ways, there were particular attributes that distinguished them from other children. There were also some instances in their childhoods that shed unexpected and revealing light upon their later years.

Taken together, the confluence of these seven stories also provides a good general idea of the kind of childhood that precedes this type of adult. That's precisely the big picture, birds-eye view this book sought to uncover: How do some children grow up to be geniuses?

My primary conclusion was that these children developed an exceptional level of self-confidence, and a strong desire to impress others — often someone special in their lives.

Confidence was required in order to ignore accepted facts dispensed by experts and ask their own questions and find their own answers.

And the need to impress others, particularly their mother or a teacher, seemed to continue as a driving impetus for their accomplishments in later life.

Surprisingly, natural intelligence didn't seem to be the main factor, but was subordinate to other factors such as passion, confidence, and persistence. In fact, sometimes these children may not have known enough to realize they were pursuing impossible goals.

The stories also provided many fascinating realizations. Some are details that helped me to better appreciate these people. And each time

I go over these stories (during my many edits) I find additional events that possibly impacted their lives.

Many of these events are small but interesting. An example is the fact that Henry Ford's father was the first one in town to have a buggy; how special did young Henry feel riding in that buggy? How much did this influence his interest in vehicles? And how did the fact that it was something most people couldn't afford contribute to his desire to make affordable cars?

In an attempt to look for things these children had in common, I added up the similar situations I found in their lives. Here are characteristics I found that three or four of them shared:

- Developed their self-confidence
- Had a childhood on a farm
- Had someone special they wanted to impress
- Had trouble staying focused
- Liked to construct dams
- Loved reading
- Suffered a tragic loss
- Their father didn't want them to go to war
- Their mother taught them to read
- Their mother was a teacher
- Was a loner
- Was bored at school
- Was fascinated by steam engines
- Was good at mathematics
- Was inquisitive
- Was shy
- Was very close to their mother

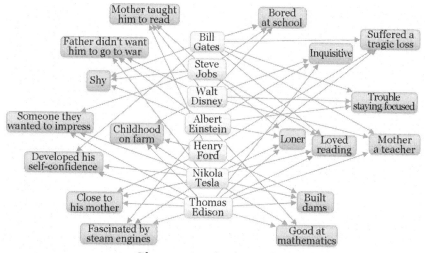

Characteristics Map

It's not that any of these characteristics actually led them to be geniuses, but some may offer insights into the development of their tenacity, curiosity, or motivation. For example, was the development of confidence a key? Or having someone special they wanted to impress? Maybe being a loner, or having a love of reading? And perhaps it was a certain combination of characteristics.

There's one more way to approach this: what characteristics did they NOT have? I can think of two: fear and boredom. None showed fear of being wrong or failing. They were attempting things no one else had done, but this challenge only encouraged them. They weren't intimidated by the possible embarrassment of failure. As they faced difficult tasks, they weren't dissuaded or hindered by some notion that they could only do "easy" things.

Neither were they bored. Yes, some things bored them but they weren't bored. When they found things that bored them, school for example, they just sidestepped them to focus on what interested them. It seemed that they were too busy chasing their dreams to ever become bored. Actually, when people complain that they're bored, they're usually just "boring," because the more interests you have, the less chance you'll have to be bored.

145

Like I said, these are my own conclusions, and yours will likely be different. But in the end, I think I now understand these people, and this type of person, in a broader and deeper way; broader by the discovery of circumstances that influenced their lives, and deeper by appreciating the emotions and motivations that propelled them.

Lessons

These stories are certainly interesting from their historical standpoint, and they're also stories most people haven't heard before. It really is fascinating to see who these amazing people were as children. But is there more to see here? Are there some useful lessons?

I think so. I think they provide an interesting perspective and understanding of our own lives and the lives of our children.

They place our own lives in a larger context, holding up a picture of what can actually be done with our lives. What are we doing with the same 24-hour days that were available to these people... people who didn't even have the advantages of our superior health, lifespan, and technology.

They also show us that the sometimes-unwanted antics and behaviors of children are possibly not simply shortcomings and quirks, but the conduct of unique individuals looking for their path.

I also noticed in these stories that sometimes children who had an apparent handicapped in one area: rebellious, inattentive, easily distracted, slow to speak, lazy, compulsive behavior, or deaf; compensated with superior abilities in others: confidence, drive, imagination, curiosity, efficiency, or inventiveness.

The basic lesson for me though is it's possible for anyone to accomplish incredible things, and although luck plays some part of every life, it's usually not the major part. It's plainly obvious that the children in these stories had to work hard and persevere to do what they did. However, I don't think they actually considered it as hard work. They had such passion in their ventures, that no matter what effort was required, it probably wasn't what they would call either "hard" or "work."

Another lesson was that of the support they received. Loving and patient parents backed them up in their endeavors and encouraged them. Some parents didn't even understand or agree with their child's preferences, but they accepted the choices they made.

I also noticed these children's uncommon disregard for rules and authority. It's not that they were disrespectful, but simply didn't automatically assume that their own ideas were inferior to others. For example, if they disagreed with classes they should attend or instructions they should follow, they simply went their own way. An independent and confident attitude allows someone to behave that way, and that kind of behavior then further reinforces the independence and confidence.

Also, none of them wallowed in self-pity or blamed others for their hardships. They accepted their lives and conditions and only applied their effort to improving them. The energy that would have been spent on pity or blame, was therefore available for them to focus more sharply on finding solutions.

They were also aggressive learners. They taught themselves what they wanted to know. In school: they weren't there to fulfill a duty, they were there to get the information they wanted... even if it wasn't the information the school intended to teach.

The overall, largest and most valuable thing I thought these stories demonstrated is that each child is extraordinarily unique, not only from other children but even from their own parents. Parents have wisdom to impart but no one is wise enough to know the innermost aspirations of another, especially of children who don't know it yet themselves. It may take children lots of zigs and zags to find their direction but this experimentation is the straightest path to their success. The more things they discover they don't like, the sooner they'll find the ones they do.

My main impression was that although children need to be protected, they don't need to be steered. They may not fit into the boxes we prepare for them, but they can thrive if we allow them to experience their own unique lives outside our expectations.

References

Researching this book required comparing several biographies. Each book and website contained portions of the childhood stories. Some stories confirmed, while others contradicted each other. It was therefore necessary to scrutinize each source of information to carefully extract the most complete and accurate stories as possible. It's understandable that legendary stories would easily accumulate around people of such mythical stature. But if this book was to be a useful description of how geniuses are raised, it needed to stick as close as possible to their true childhoods.

The following are the books found to be the most useful. The internet was also a source of additional details and a helpful resource for sleuthing out fact from fiction. If you're interested, these books also offer an excellent way to follow "the rest of the story."

Bill Gates

- Bill Gates: A Biography — bit.ly/Gates-01
- Who Is Bill Gates? — bit.ly/Gates-02
- Bill Gates: The Life, Lessons & Rules for Success — bit.ly/Gates-03
- Bill Gates biography — bit.ly/Gates-04
- The Biography of Bill Gates — bit.ly/Gates-05
- Bill Gates: Digital Mastermind — bit.ly/Gate-06
- Bill Gates — bit.ly/Gates-07
- Bill Gates: A Biography — bit.ly/Gates-08
- Bill Gates: Entrepreneur and Philanthropist — bit.ly/Gates-09

Steve Jobs

- Steve Jobs — bit.ly.com/SJobs-01
- Steve Jobs: The Man Who Thought Different — bit.ly.com/SJobs-02
- Who Was Steve Jobs? — bit.ly.com/SJobs-03
- Steve Jobs: Thinking Differently — bit.ly.com/SJobs-04
- Steve Jobs: American Genius — bit.ly.com/SJobs-05
- Steve Jobs: The Journey is the Reward — bit.ly.com/SJobs-06
- Steve Jobs: The Unauthorized Autobiography — bit.ly.com/SJobs-07
- Steve Jobs: An Icon to Remember — bit.ly.com/SJobs-08
- The Bite in the Apple: A Memoir of My Life with Steve Jobs — bit.ly.com/SJobs-09

Walt Disney

- Walt Disney — bit.ly.com/Disney-01
- Walt Disney: Hollywood's Dark Prince — bit.ly.com/Disney-02
- The Story of Walt Disney: Maker of Magical Worlds — bit.ly.com/Disney-03
- LIFE Walt Disney: From Mickey to the Magic Kingdom — bit.ly.com/Disney-04
- Disney — bit.ly.com/Disney-05
- The Animated Man: A Life of Walt Disney — bit.ly.com/Disney-06
- Young Walt Disney: A Biography of Walt Disney's Younger Years — bit.ly.com/Disney-07

Albert Einstein

- Einstein: A Life of Genius — bit.ly/Einstein-01
- Albert Einstein: The Life of a Genius — bit.ly/Einstein-02
- Einstein: A Biography — bit.ly/Einstein-03
- Albert Einstein: A Life from Beginning to End — bit.ly/Einstein-04
- Albert Einstein: Father of The Modern Scientific Age — bit.ly/Einstein-05
- Albert Einstein: The Biography of a Genius — bit.ly/Einstein-06
- Einstein: His Life and Universe — bit.ly/Einstein-07
- Einstein: A Biography — bit.ly/Einstein-08

Henry Ford

- I Invented the Modern Age: The Rise of Henry Ford — bit.ly.com/Ford-01
- The People's Tycoon: Henry Ford and the American Century — bit.ly.com/Ford-02
- Henry Ford — bit.ly.com/Ford-03
- Who Was Henry Ford? — bit.ly.com/Ford-04
- My Life and Work: Autobiography of Henry Ford — bit.ly.com/Ford-05
- American Legends: The Life of Henry Ford — bit.ly.com/Ford-06
- Henry Ford's Own Story — bit.ly.com/Ford-07

Nikola Tesla

- Master of Electricity - Nikola Tesla — bit.ly/Tesla-01
- Wizard: The Life and Times of Nikola Tesla — bit.ly/Tesla-02
- Tesla: Inventor of the Electrical Age — bit.ly/Tesla-03
- Nikola Tesla: A Captivating Guide to the Life of a Genius Inventor — bit.ly/Tesla-04
- Nikola Tesla: Prophet of The Modern Technological Age — bit.ly/Tesla-05
- Prodigal Genius: The Life of Nikola Tesla — bit.ly/Tesla-06
- Nikola Tesla: The Imagination and Man — bit.ly/Tesla-07

Thomas Edison

- Who Was Thomas Alva Edison? — bit.ly/Edison-01
- Edison: His Life and Inventions — bit.ly/Edison-02
- Thomas Edison: American Inventor — bit.ly/Edison-03
- Thomas Edison: Inspiration and Hard Work — bit.ly/Edison-04
- Thomas Edison: Thomas Edison's Inventions — bit.ly/Edison-05
- Young Thomas Edison — bit.ly/Edison-06
- Thomas Edison for Kids: His Life and Ideas — bit.ly/Edison-07
- Wizard of Menlo Park - Thomas Edison — bit.ly/Edison-08
- Thomas Edison: The Biography — bit.ly/Edison-09
- The Life and Inventions of Edison — bit.ly/Edison-10

Your Review

I hope you enjoyed this book. If you did, please leave a review on Amazon. This is the only way Amazon will notice that the book is worth promoting. Indie book publishing is a competitive field, and you the reader have the most control over a book's success. So, if you can leave a review, here's a short link to the review page: bit.ly/FTWC-Review.

If this book is well-received, it would be fun to do another, so please write if you have suggestions for people to include in a possible sequel.

Thanks again, and I hope you had as much fun as I did.

About the Author

David Butler is a retired mechanical engineer, who when he's not annoying his beautiful Colombian wife, enjoys reading, playing with 360° photography, and virtual reality. If you have any feedback or comments on these stories (or helpful tips on writing) he can be reached at email@davidbutler.us.

33642948R00086

Made in the USA
San Bernardino, CA
24 April 2019